An Existential Manifesto

SONDER

VIPULESH THIYAGARAJAH

ISBN: 979-8-9909280-1-5 (Paperback)
ISBN: 979-8-9909280-2-2 (Hardcover)
ISBN: 979-8-9909280-0-8 (E-Book)

Book cover design and interior formatting by 100Covers.

First printing edition 2024.

To my father, Veeriah Thiyagarajah.

*Who will probably skip this section
if nobody tells him about it.*

CONTENTS

An Existential Manifesto

SONDER

PART ONE

FOUNDATIONS

CHAPTER 1

THE VALUE OF THOUGHT

"Very little is needed to make a happy life;
it is all within yourself, in your way of thinking."
- Marcus Aurelius

For the last few millennia, humanity has been facing a dilemma, mostly of their own doing: Our struggles to cope with the ever-evolving complexities of life and achieve a state of constant fulfillment, dubbed 'happiness.' As relieving as it may seem to be reassured that eternal bliss can be found within oneself by leading a simplistic routine and cultivating a philosophical mind, the reality is that self-actualization, for a sentient being that operates within the weaves of societal intricacies, is nigh impossible.

In today's social landscape, it is imperative to understand that your quality of life, emotional and physical, depends heavily on externalities, on a micro and macro scale of externally defined social constructs, just as much as any internal factors. The unpopular truth of the world is that we are cursed in many ways, a species chosen by natural selection to thrive through suffering and unequivocal interdependence... a species plagued by consciousness.

The Curse of Consciousness

The Curse of Consciousness is a hypothesis that mankind is eternally damned by the evolutionary path that led to our capacity to think through time, confined by our past, the forgotten present, and the dreaded unpredictability of a fearful future. The very ability to perceive history, comprehend our present in the third person, and account for the future is an evolutionary edge that humans have exploited in our rise in the natural order. It revolutionizes the way we look at the world, helping us understand that our ability to process information in various departments is what sets us apart from primal beings who only possess the ability to 'think' as opposed to being conscious.

Homosapiens possess what psychologists refer to as an 'autobiographical consciousness,' that predominantly perceives our past and future as critical drivers for problem-solving and abstract analysis. This is in contrast to primitive life, which relies heavily on core consciousness, such as instinct and impulses, to drive their thoughts and decisions. The further the void between homo-sapiens and unadulterated human nature, the more advanced the effects of the Curse of Consciousness.

According to Professor D. Wickremasinghe, the core purpose of human consciousness is Preservation, Accumulation, and Interconnectedness. To achieve this, our brain operates in three modes: Drive, Safe, and Threat.

The Drive Brain is responsible for Accumulation, such as competition, adventurousness, achievement, and all neurological responses that motivate a winning mentality. It is the core feature that fuels the fire for power and the drive to be better than the rest of your peers.

The Safe Brain is the harbinger of peace and promotes rest, relaxation, social relatability, and complex thinking on a multifaceted approach. These traits enable humanity to satisfy tasks such as reproduction and social interaction through the multitude of networks and relationships formed over one's lifetime.

The most overactive prong of the core characteristics of the brain's psychology is the Threat Brain, which enables the recognition and response to perceived danger. The single most important instinct that we are incapable of avoiding is self-preservation.

In equilibrium, the three brains regulate the motivational system of an evolved primate—like a checks-and-balances system designed to eliminate the possibility of one prong claiming dominance over others, rendering the human incapable of optimal cognitive performance.

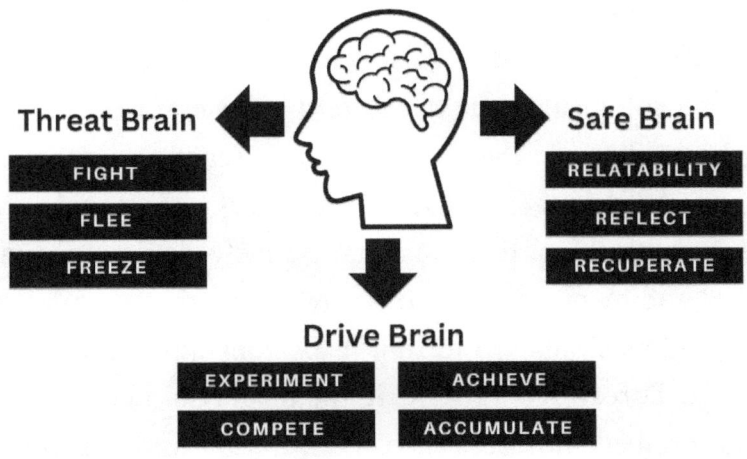

The 21st century witnessed an assortment of crises; in the twenty-five years since the beginning of the millennium, we have outlived the dot com crash, the housing market bubble, the Covid-19 pandemic, annexations, terrorism, and numerous wars, but a segment of the most destructive crises of the modern era remain underestimated and understated. The epidemic of depression, anxiety, and suicide, alongside the declining mental well-being of many, has quietly permeated the collective consciousness, proliferating as a result of humanity's inclination to attribute instability in the status quo to external factors rather than internal ones.

The key culprit of all the verbiage above is a disintegrated motivational system and a hyperactive Threat Brain. It has been shown that overactivity in the Threat Brain directly correlates to an individual's habitual behavior, environment, and social standing. The Threat Brain induces stress in our system, the fight-or-flight response, provoking the amygdala (also known as the fear center in your neurological organs), triggering a plethora of bodily responses that are then observed as a reaction; increased heart rate, elevated cortisol levels (stress hormone), and many physical implications that actively deplete physiological and mental energy to create a sensation that can be described as similar to feeling ill. A constantly active and engaged Threat Brain results in the display of behaviors of stress-induced illnesses, such as initiating and sustaining conflict, communication avoidance, and over-compliance, which can have detrimental effects on an individual's mental health and personal life. These behaviors can lead to a range of distressing problems, like addiction, chronic anxiety, shame, loneliness, depression, and even suicide.

The contrast between an animal's Threat Brain function and the evolved modern humans is our ability to perceive threats through time. We are tormented by the distant memories of danger that can reincarnate themselves in conceptualized contexts, and we imagine perceived threats far into the future that may have no probability of materializing. Your brain, however, acknowledges all threats, past, present, or future, through the mechanism of the Threat Brain, causing all the neurological, chemical, and physical reactions to trigger, reigniting effects of perpetual anxiousness due to the curse of our consciousness.

Compassion Fatigue and Hyperfixation are predominant tells of the aforementioned condition, in addition to anxiety and stress, for personnel with dysregulated neural motivation. Compassion fatigue is the inability to empathize due to frequent exposure to a particular element. It is prevalent in medicinal practitioners and police officers who are regularly exposed to situations that evoke empathy in people. Hyperfixation is when a person concentrates heavily on a particular distraction that enables them to remove thoughts of all other variables affecting them. An example is workaholism; people dive headfirst into their careers or a time-consuming project to avoid mourning or grieving over an unfortunate event. This human condition even materializes in your weekend escape to the golf course to avert a partner or the attempted prevention of loneliness by being overly social and surrounding oneself with a crowd at all times. Through suppression, we allow ourselves to relive unresolved trauma from the past as our brain begins to acclimatize to a chronic state of the 'fight or flight' response through compassion fatigue, overexposure to anxiousness, and constant threat responses. These behavior patterns facilitate inflexibility and harmful tendencies, furthering disequilibrium with the Drive Brain, Safe Brain, and Threat Brain.

As part and parcel of the most integrated and interdependent society in the history of humanity, I believe the increase in activity with regard to the function of the Threat Brain is at an unprecedented high. Its overstimulation renders the Safe Brain underutilized and reprogrammes the Drive Brain to function at a toxic level that fosters a culture of 'threat-motivated achievement.' This is evident through the rise in capitalism and competitive culture that only rewards winning, hegemony, and a constant accumulation of wealth and power. Misplaced ambition and widespread misinformation fuel self-induced feelings of inadequacy and unworthiness, taking the wheel and becoming core motivation. A type of toxic drive in fear of social vulnerability and societal incompetence, making each and every single one of us a ticking time bomb, primed for implosion from within.

But like all curses, this, too, is breakable. To begin, one should play the cards they are dealt because no one flops the nuts every time. Humans are not inclined to fold when the hands they are dealt are sub-optimal. They have been conditioned to do anything to ensure survival and a considerable part of that is being able to respond to danger and threat. The cultivation of the skills and ability to identify genuine, unimagined threats and all other obstacles you would need to navigate through your problems is the first step in regulating your ability to control the motivational drivers of your brain. It is ok to tense up, pass judgment, be overly critical, and even imagine scenarios where your significant other is cheating on you or how you will save the day by landing a commercial airplane if both pilots suddenly died mid-journey. Recognizing and acknowledging these thoughts, however, is the only path forward. Self-awareness and being able to train yourself to detect your throat closing up, muscles tensing, and mind rendering improbable mirages to reality is the way to regulate your hypersensitive Threat Brain. A firm grasp of the present and being grounded in the moment may be humanity's only hope in escaping this epidemic.

While we cope with the existential dread of chronic mental turmoil, the very consciousness that we are cursed with may also be the greatest blessing that we could have hoped for. That is what the remainder of this novel will address: A way of life, habits, environment, culture, and social constructs that serve as a compass to harnessing the capacity to comprehend one's mental and social consciousness and its shades of complications. The book will dive deeper into factors that are pertinent to the abilities mentioned above, the effect that people around us have on us, the understanding of one's own emotions, the history of society, how mimetic theory shapes the psyche of all individuals, and even the rise and fall of empires and the role they play as an external force in all our lives.

The Allegory of the Cave

Plato's Cave, also referred to as the allegory of the cave, is a philosophical interpretation of the effects of education and the lack of it in our nature. To be less cryptic, the Cave is a message to the world; as Plato put it, "It is the task of the enlightened not only to ascend to learning and to see the good but to be willing to descend again to those prisoners and to share their troubles and their honors, whether they are worth having or not. And this they must do, even with the prospect of death."

The image symbolizes society's constructs and the invisible hand that controls the world. The enlightened are simply human beings who have achieved emotional and situational awareness, which enables them to escape the shackles of the Cave and truly be free.

To understand the image, look to the left wall that projects shadows of objects manipulated by puppet masters hidden behind a wall. Facing the wall are people chained and left immobile since childhood. Socrates argues that the shadows on the wall are interpreted as reality by all the prisoners who stare at it. And to those poor souls, that is their only truth; the visible world is the creation of the mere reflection in their immediate vicinity, yet that is the extent of their intellectual comprehension.

The Cave offers a retrospective view of humanity's path and human nature's evolution. People shackled within the Cave bear witness to a false sense of reality of an inconsistent world, separated from the truth, like the wall that divided the puppet masters and the masses. The people who refuse to question their beliefs and fallacies, those who are unable to engage in healthy discourse, self-improvement, self-reflection, and curiously questioning every aspect of their life, may never come to enjoy the unequivocal truth of their reality. Those eternally damned will continue to remain in the dark depths of the Cave, with no idea of the endless possibilities of existence outside of the confines and comfort of ignorant bliss.

Meanwhile, the other end of the spectrum, the enlightened, with new experiences and knowledge under their belt, would never be able to return to their former ways of life and associate with the players of the old culture. The person who left the Cave may also come to pity, or even feel superior, judgemental, to those who have not escaped. The enlightened may be compelled to aid those within the Cave but will permanently be expunged from their former social structure by the very people that they hoped to rescue, cursed to a life of suffering with the consciousness they chose to cultivate.

When I was first introduced to the allegory of the Cave, I was thrown a curve ball in the form of religion. The opposing argument was: What if the enlightened were religious folk who escaped the enclosure and fallacies of capitalism and modern scientific ideologies? Their position would then be of those who truly understood the meaning of life through an omnipotent being and divine scripture, a separate parallel to scientific enlightenment.

This, frankly, left me stumped and unable to justify Plato's philosophy. It seemed contradictory to what I believed: that I was seeking enlightenment and escaping the Cave through education, experience, cultural immersion, and scientific discovery. What if I was the narrow-minded prisoner, caught up in modern belief, misguided, and naive?

Then again, isn't that the point of the Cave? To question one's reality and to further question the rationale of their thoughts, emotions, and norms? Every unique individual is differentiated not only by their DNA but also by mutually exclusive experiences that form personality and shape divergent consciousness. The path to freedom, enlightenment, and truth is not fixed but somewhat variable and endless. Unbound by time and space, limited by none other than your own capacity to be curious and non-judgemental of the path that you have chosen to take as opposed to another. The sonder path of humanity.

Sonder

"n. the realization that each random passerby is living a life as vivid and complex as your own—populated with their own ambitions, friends, routines, worries, and in-herited craziness—an epic story that continues invisibly around you like an anthill sprawling deep underground, with elaborate passageways to thousands of other lives that you'll never know existed, in which you might appear only once, as an extra sipping coffee in the background, as a blur of traffic passing on the highway, as a lighted window at dusk."

I discovered a coffee shop called 'Sonder' in Cape Town, South Africa. The place was as hipster as it sounds; baristas worshiped their craft, the smell of freshly roast-ed coffee beans drowned your senses, and lightly blotted leather seats had decades of history etched onto the stains. A modern interpretation of native African art decorated the walls, and the occasional crush of a warm croissant broke the silence instituted by the in-house library, gov-erned by an honor system. A peculiar place, filled with fascinating people.

In my 2 brief months in the region, I couldn't possibly name a local dweller I had the privilege of meeting who wasn't unapologetically in love with their life. In spite of your average global economic hardship, working-class strains, and other omnipresent issues, every South African I spoke to shared a sense of underlying happiness and calm. I didn't understand the elegance they possessed in navigating the craziness of day-to-day life with... grace. They owned their colonial history and made it a part and parcel of their identities. They learned from their past but did not let the bitter aftertaste of history affect their considerations for and relationship with all people in their immediate vicinity, no matter how divergent their beliefs, intellectual proficiency, or the color of their skin. While issues are very much prevalent in the country, it appeared to me that people strove for mimetic matrimony with one another, and the by-product of it all was happiness, not everlasting, but a perpetual stream of peace, social prosperity, and conscious bliss.

So what was it? Their secret to everlasting happiness, or so it may seem. It was right before me, not a shadow cast on a wall, but an authentic reality of the truth behind it all. Unlike Marcus Aurelius, I don't think happiness comes from within! You alone cannot be the only source of your joy. The blessing of consciousness can only be achieved through an equilibrium between you and your environment. Your social standing, community, culture, relationships, experience, and exposure all weigh heavily on your capacity to be physically and mentally in balance... to achieve, if not achieve, but at least come remotely close to the destination of our noble pursuit of happiness... self-actualization.

So, was our highly developed sense of consciousness a blessing or a curse? It depends on your perspective.

"Life is a tragedy when seen in close-up, but a comedy in long-shot."
- Charlie Chaplin.

CHAPTER 2

THE PURSUIT OF HAPPINESS

You will never be happy! Let me explain.

We must first understand what happiness is when aspiring to uncover humanity's most prolific search, the perpetual strive to achieve a state of permanent, unadulterated joy. Is it a feeling? Is it your Ivy League degree hung up on the wall, outlined by a gold-plated frame that reminds all your colleagues that you are superior? Is it your beautiful high school sweetheart that you've been dating for 27 years and is now your wife? Is it retirement, money, cars, or a belief?

Happiness is not a feeling. Happiness is merely an impermanent state of being, like hunger or the pain you feel when you stub your toe on the side of a piece of furniture. A momentary sense of Satisfaction, Purpose, and Enjoyment: The three prongs of what contributes to your sense of 'feeling happy.'

Perhaps you disagree. I may be wrong, along with every divergent theory attempting to simplify and decisively define the concept. Still, one thing we can all collectively agree on is that happiness is always associated with positive emotions. It is used to characterize an individual's subjective emotional well-being on a holistic scale. Aristotle classifies the phenomena as a sense of receiving or achieving a desire through instant gratification, comparative success, positive communal contributions, and even self-actualization.

Aristotle goes on to split happiness into two kinds: Eudaimonia and Hedonia. The direct translation of Eudaimonia reads - "conducive to happiness," an interpretation I connect to very much. Eudaimonia is the noble sense of purpose, and a chronic search for purpose is a driving source for the human battery. An eternal search for meaning in your existence is dramatic yet romantic and equally benevolent when considering how inconsequential you may be in the grand scheme of things, to find comfort in the discovery of virtue and the significance of one's consciousness and physical embodiment in a sea of billions on the same noble pursuit.

Hedonia, conversely, is to feed our primal instincts by deriving happiness from pleasure. Self-love, travel the world, enjoy your life, the 'do what gives you joy' mentality. And that seems quite comprehensive - do what you love, make a positive difference, and find a sense of purpose. Yet that isn't everything. Why is the world so miserable if it is as trivial as the premise above? Why are we, in the 21st century, in a depression epidemic?

The reason lies in the fact that we have forgotten to take pleasure in our suffering.

For centuries, humanity has unanimously understood that life is an endless stream of suffering. Religious texts, ancient philosophers of Greece, and even politicians and soldiers reached a common consensus when it came to this. They agreed upon an ideology that pain, suffering, mistakes, setbacks, heartbreak, competition, and even death are all pertinent to development. Through experiential maturity, we can learn to appreciate the hard-earned state of relief, enjoyment, satisfaction, and growth. But somewhere along the way, we lost the want, the will to fight, and somehow decided to settle for mainstream mediocrity. We chose to coddle and protect children, teenagers, and now adults from hardship, making them ill-suited to stay accountable and deal with the consequences of their choices and uncontrollable externalities. We forsake effort when faced with adversity and blame the world for the unfair societal constructs that have made it nearly improbable to excel. We refuse to suffer today for a better tomorrow and grow to love instant gratification, hoping that it will all compound into an imagined rendition of happiness. Yet somewhere along this path, we chose to become victims of struggle rather than embracing it as the natural procession to a prosperous tomorrow.

History is a reminder that suffering is equally present in every conscious being. To know joy, you need to know sorrow and grief. To understand physical strength, you once had to be weak, grow strength, and eventually be weakened again by age. The only reason we value life is due to the undisputed fact that death is foreseeable, even imminent. The rich mourn their demise, the impoverished starve, the protectors suffer injury, and the providers work endlessly. We all have our individualized forms of hardship. That is not to say that you should simply endure the brute force of the world with open arms, but you could accept its unavoidable presence with an open mind.

Prior to the 18th century, happiness had to be earned through ascension in social ranks. This, of course, was subjective to the standard of living at the time. A secure home, financial standing, ability to ward off disease, the luxury of bearing offspring in a sanitary or medical environment, and overall affordability of healthcare were all markers of a satisfied family. Happiness was viewed as a state of living, a privilege earned rather than given, to which anyone and everyone was entitled. What were once considered luxuries turned into necessities through programs such as healthcare, the internet network, transportation infrastructure, forms of financial credit, and the general globalization of the planet, elevating everyone's quality of life. The question remains, however: If we live significantly more lavish, privileged lives than most noblemen and high society individuals who seemingly lived happier lives in the past, how are we continuing to show exponentially higher rates of decline in happiness and mental fortitude with more resources and social/physical securities of the modern world?

$$\text{SATISFACTION} = \frac{\text{WHAT YOU HAVE}}{\text{WHAT YOU WANT}}$$

To put it relatively crudely, we care about too much shit, we want too much stuff, and we know too many things about things that happen everywhere. To put it in a mathematical equation, according to Professor Arthur C. Brooks, your satisfaction is a coefficient of 'what you have' and 'what you want.'

As humanity developed proficiency in providing necessities and satisfying the needs of the masses, we learned to focus on our wants, training ourselves to gauge our satisfaction, purpose, and enjoyment through short-term gratifications in bipolar scales. Emotional states were judged based on whether one was momentarily happy or not. Homosapiens are capable of a spectrum of emotions and can feel in a multitude of intensities. Yet we grew further and further distant from neutrality in search of the polar ends of our feelings.

"If I'm not happy, then it must mean I'm supposed to feel sad."

"Sad is bad."

"Negative feelings must mean that I'm an unhappy person?"

Right?

Not exactly.

We associate feelings of shame, sadness, fear, anxiety, and the like as negative thoughts, and that your well-being depends on not feeling these emotions over positive alternatives. Your brain, however, produces happiness, pleasure, and joy from a completely different hemisphere than depression, anger, and dissatisfaction because the negative emotions listed in the latter part of the sentence are evolutionary feelings that have intensified to keep you alive. They are the modern renditions of the Threat Brain, adapting you to combat the circumstances of your immediate environment, and should be seen as good reactions rather than bad ones. Still, having 'things you want' supersede the 'things you have' is a direct cause of overstimulation; you feel increased intensities of the supposedly 'negative' feelings, worsening your quality of life. The equation above does not promote an increase in 'what you have' by any means, which can be equally detrimental to one's well-being. Instead, the point is to train yourself to reduce the disparity between the numerator and the denominator to achieve a state of homeostasis.

Homeostasis - "*n. The natural process of self-regulation by which an organism maintains stability while adapting to the most favorable conditions for survival. Homeostasis is the tendency towards a relatively stable state of balance between interdependent elements, especially as maintained by physiological processes. When homeostasis is successful, the organism continues to thrive, but if it fails, it can result in disaster or even death.*"

The Hedonic Treadmill

The hedonic treadmill is a concept coined by Philip Brickman and Donald T. Campbell, who researched the emotional effect and the return to homeostasis on human beings regarding emotional divergence. No matter the stage of life they may be in, their levels of success, personal experiences, or their surroundings, an individual will possess a stable emotional state, known as the baseline. Any intense, positive, or negative emotion will cause a person's emotional state to diverge from the baseline. The effect of homeostasis, however, will return them to their natural levels of emotional equilibrium over a variable period.

Two factors contribute to this phenomenon: adaptation and comparison.

Adaptation is our natural tendency to acclimatize to new experiences, reducing the positive or negative effects of an event, possession, or person on our emotional affect over steady and constant exposure. Driving a brand-new Mercedes off the lot is a euphoric experience for some; sooner or later, you've driven it a couple of times, dented the front bumper on your driveway, and had your newborn baby use the back seats as a personal urinal, and you don't receive the same sense of pleasure and enjoyment of driving the car as you did when you got it.

This effect is called the law of diminishing marginal utility, where the satisfaction derived from consuming a good or service declines after a certain threshold. For example, your favorite slice of pizza, eaten every day, will eventually make you sick of the very thing you once craved.

LAW OF DIMINISHING MARGINAL UTILITY

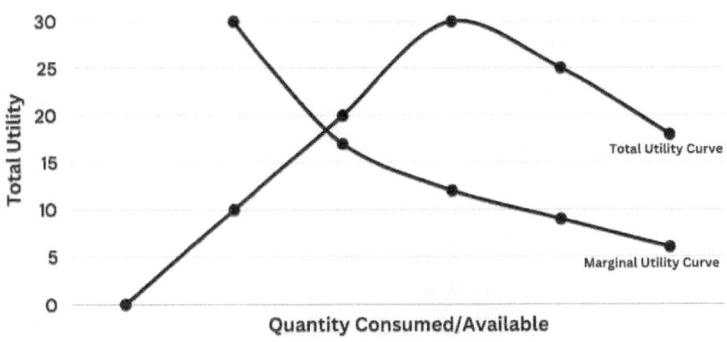

On the other hand, comparison occurs when we experience reduced satisfaction from a particular entity due to the comparative satisfaction we gain from another individual. In other words, we feel worse about our lives and what we have when we see someone else be better off. With the broad reach of social media, we are constantly comparing our lifestyle with that of millions, even billions of others. This effect is continuously experienced, increasingly, and overwhelmingly, causing hyperinflated insecurities, feelings of unworthiness, dissatisfaction with achievements, and hindering your solitary growth, impeding all the factors stereotypically needed to be 'happy.'

Now add the effects of comparison and adaptation with the impact of an endlessly growing collection of "wants" that supersedes anything that may be obtainable for your circumstance. The result will be an overactive Threat Brain that makes you feel all intensities of emotions, such as anxiety, shame, and a plethora of other unpleasant feelings.

The strongest minds among us will not be able to tolerate such hyperactivity in the brain for a prolonged duration. Typical coping mechanisms default towards adoring material possessions, power, money, popularity, and anything and everything that will provide instant gratification to avoid reverting to homeostasis. This level of intensity in dopamine recurrence will prolong the half-life of your return to baseline: Chasing happiness, never satisfied, never in balance. So you keep running on the treadmill, constantly, faster, faster yet again, until your natural equilibrium point is forgotten, lost, or unpalatable to your conscience. This will ultimately result in you falling off the treadmill, crashing, and imploding from within.

According to a study conducted by Deiner and a group of researchers, individuals can have non-neutral set points of homeostasis. The study found that most people have a steady state of above-neutral affect balance score, which calculates the positive or negative emotions felt beyond a specified equilibrium point. For most people, their baseline state tends to be one of well-being.

However, if an individual is constantly exposed to adverse circumstances that evoke unpleasant emotions, their baseline tends to be lower than those who experience mostly pleasant occurrences. Despite this, most people tend to revert to a neutral state and consistently report a positive effect on their emotional state, regardless of their financial situation, physical appearance, or health-related standing.

For example, consider individuals who belong to the physically disabled community and have undergone significant life-altering events, such as the loss of limbs or blindness. When their emotional affect scores were calculated, they displayed similar levels of positive emotional well-being as perfectly healthy individuals after having had time to acclimate to their new state of life. This indicates that our consciousness is adaptive, enabling us to return to a positive affect level close to our biological homeostasis. The ability to accept this phenomenon is dependent on metacognition.

Metacognition

n. 'Metacognition refers to a person's ability to recognize and comprehend their thinking patterns. The term meta, which means "beyond" or "on top of," forms the basis of this word. In essence, metacognition is the process of reflecting on one's thoughts, recognizing them, and controlling them.'

Deiner goes on to explain that personality has a strong correlation to well-being. A person's personality factors predispose them to experience alternate levels of well-being irrespective of life events due to their instinctual reaction. Metacognition also encompasses the ability to be critically aware of one's thinking, self-question, self-reflect, be mindful of one's strengths and weaknesses, and evaluate one's feelings.

Your feelings, as abstract as they may be, can broadly be quantified by The Positive and Negative Affect Schedule (PANAS) test, which measures emotional affect. It consists of a multiple-choice questionnaire that can be completed in 2 minutes, and a clinically agreed-upon result will be produced to determine your affect schedule.

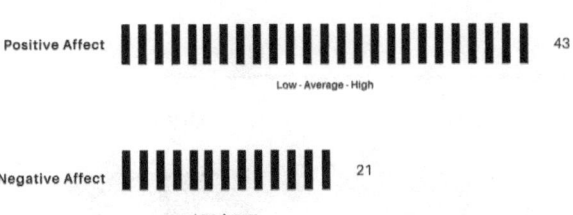

This evaluation can be used to group yourself into four subsets of traits: High Positive, High Negative, Low Positive, and Low Negative. The following analysis will explain the four different subcategories of emotional affect. I recommend taking the PANAS test before proceeding.

Arthur C. Brooks has classified people into four segments: the Mad Scientist, the Judge, the Cheerleader, and the Poet. You fall into the Cheerleader category if you tend to express many positive and very few negative emotions. If you tend to indicate a lot of negative emotional affect and low positive affect, you are a Poet. This means that you might find yourself in a bad mood more often than in a good one. If you experience high levels of both positive and negative emotions, you are a Mad Scientist. You encounter a lot of strong emotions, both good and bad. If you have low levels of both positive and negative affect, you are a Judge, headstrong, and don't experience many strong emotions on either extreme.

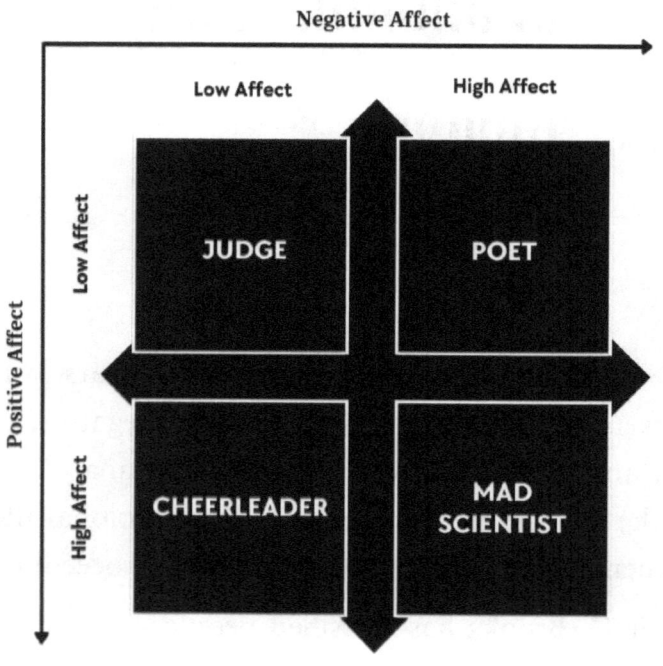

These traits are neither good nor bad but rather a characterization of your tendencies. Your ability to be metacognitive will enable you to find a happy median between self-destructive, self-fulfilling, high affective, and low affective.

From seeing the charts above, most people will instinctively prefer to be a cheerleader or at least have cheerleaders around them. Wouldn't life be fantastic if you have low negative affect and high positive affect, feeling psychologically blissful at all times? A delighted individual with low negativity and hyper-cooperative tendencies lacks the negative triad of Machiavellianism, narcissism, and psychopathy. They are the adrenaline junkies, the explorers, the 'live your life to the fullest' kind of people - the type that Nike or Red Bull would put on their ads. It seems like a great trait to have in a life partner, am I right?

Cheerleaders aren't as great as they may seem at first glance. These personality types are threat-avoidant and exhibit strong reactions to perceived danger. They cannot take bad news, will avoid difficulty, and lack emotional stability. They may be overly social and extraverted, almost people pleasing, easily manipulated, tend to be compensated poorly due to their inability to negotiate under duress, and show signs of low-stress tolerance. They also tend to be highly spiritual – the astrology and numerology kind. They tend to move around a lot, are never stable, and are never in one place, scientifically known as high locomotion. Despite looking good on paper, the truth of the matter is that being a cheerleader is not as glamorous as it appears.

Judges have a low positive and low negative affect. They fit perfectly in high-stress professions due to their tendency to not feel or react to emotions with great intensity. This inherently means that they will have better impulse control and emotional maturity. Judges don't necessarily struggle with depression or anxiety but also aren't overly social, cooperative, or extroverted. These folk are usually the perfect CEOs, negotiators, surgeons, or any job that involves high stakes. And yes, they will kick your ass at poker.

The Poet is self-destructive, introverted, highly neurotic, always scheming, lacks empathy, and is threat-avoidant and selfish. They tend to be worse off psychologically and indicate poor overall well-being. As the name suggests, Poets are the creatives and the romantics. It may seem unfavorable to be a 'Poet,' but they possess the best qualities of the 'Judge' without the downfalls of a cheerleader. A 'Poet' with positive affect is a great asset.

The Mad Scientist exhibits a high affect across all metrics. They feel intensity on all spectrums, both positive and negative. They have a sense of mastery about their environment, show tremendous personal growth, and tend to seek self-actualization. They value autonomy and harmony. A true master of metacognition. However, they hold incredible ambitions as a result of self-objectification and a crippling fear of failure, usually resulting in workaholism, high stress, and psychophysiological issues. 'Mad Scientists' are cocky – confident, arrogant, but self-directed. They are not self-transcendent, but manipulative, unsympathetic, calculative, threat avoidant, and heavily reward dependent.

HIGH POSITIVE AFFECT

SELF-FULFILLING

- High levels of psychological well-being.
- High levels of subjective well-being: life satisfaction, high positive affect, low negative affect, and harmony.
- Low levels of ill-being: low depressive and stress symptoms.
- Personality: low in neuroticism, high in extraversion, low in harm avoidance, high in persistence, high in self-directedness, high in cooperativeness, low in machiavellianism, psychopathy, and narcissism.
- Other: physically active, spiritual behavior, high energy and locomotion, low in rumination.

HIGH AFFECTIVE

- High levels of psychological well-being: environmental mastery, self-acceptance, personal growth, and purpose in life.
- Low levels of psychological well-being: autonomy.
- High levels of subjective well-being: life satisfaction and harmony.
- Low levels of ill-being: low depressive symptoms.
- High levels of ill-being: psychophysiological problems and stress.
- Personality: high in neuroticism, extroverted, harm avoidant, reward dependent, self-directed, low in self-transcendence, high in machiavellianism, psychopathy, and narcissism.
- Other: physically active, high energy and locomotion, high in remuneration.

LOW NEGATIVE AFFECT

HIGH NEGATIVE AFFECT

LOW AFFECTIVE

- High levels of psychological well-being.
- High subjective well-being: life satisfaction and harmony.
- Low levels of ill-being: low depressive and stress symptoms.
- High levels of ill-being: high psycho-physiological and sleeping problems.
- Personality: low in extraversion, high in emotional stability, low in persistence, low in self-directedness, low in co-operativeness, low machiavellianism, psychopathy, and narcissism).
- Other: not physically active, low energy and locomotion, high in remuneration.

SELF-DESTRUCTIVE

- Low levels of psychological well-being.
- Low levels of subjective well-being.
- High levels of ill-being: high depressive & stress symptoms, regular psycho-physiological and sleeping problems.
- Personality: high in introversion, high in neuroticism, low persistence, harm avoidance, low self-directedness, low co-operativeness, high machiavellianism, psychopathy, and narcissism.
- Other: not physically active, low energy and locomotion, high in rumination, low in spirituality.

LOW POSITIVE AFFECT

The Reverse Bucket List

A conventional bucket list is an array of all your life's desires. It typically consists of one's hopes, dreams, and desires reduced to several bullet points. And if you're anything like me, that list is ever-evolving and ever-expanding. I learned of the Reverse Bucket List in a TED Talk by Arthur C. Brooks. In his speech, Brooks surprisingly claimed that having a typical bucket list is counterproductive to your happiness. He said a bucket list was a constant reminder of what you want in life, as opposed to all the incredible things you have achieved.

We all intuitively want to do aspirational things, and don't get me wrong—having long-term goals does indeed give you a sense of purpose and provides much-needed direction in life. Everyone wants to make a million dollars, get promoted, visit the world's wonders, and so on. Scientific research backs the claim that striving to check off things on your list might give you momentary joy when you achieve said goal, a euphoric high indicating a sense of accomplishment.

It stands to reason that if we agree with what has been said so far, our brains will adjust to dopamine levels, compare our achievements with others, and eventually return to a baseline emotional state. So yes, at that very moment, you will feel fulfilled, but in the blink of an eye, that feeling will be gone, and you will hop back on that treadmill because the next carrot is being dangled right over your nose in the form of a predetermined bucket list.

Evaluate your list. Write down everything you've wanted to do, wanted to possess, gain, and then reflect on the item. What kind of desires or wants are they? Does its inclusion provide a positive impact on your life in the long run? Is it a material desire? Power? Money? A taste for the pleasures of the skin? Think about how achieving those checkboxes on that piece of paper will elevate your vision of yourself in five, ten, or maybe fifteen years.

If you genuinely believe that the item on that list will bring you mental peace and push you closer to more satisfaction, purpose, and enjoyment, then do it. If you suddenly notice a change of heart about that goal you set for yourself, subtract it from your list. It gives you one less thing to want, pulling you closer to the equilibrium between what you have and what you want.

By no means am I encouraging you not to do the things you want. Most people grow to resent the time they didn't spend just having fun instead of caring so much about all the minor technicalities in their past:

- The nights spent studying instead of partying.
- The vacation you bailed on to save money for a condo.

- The business you procrastinated on for years.

- The girl you let slip away because you didn't want to make an effort.

All regrets you need not have if you follow a 'carpe diem' attitude. And to be honest, that is perfectly fine, too. Be the cheerleader; we all need to be one occasionally. You're not expected to be the perfect embodiment of balance and emotional competence at all times. However, being actively aware of why you do things is important. Question the judgment calls you make. Be critical of your goals and aspirations, and do them for the right reasons, not for the sake of validation, instant gratification, or material wealth. This will help you cultivate a metacognitive mind, control your point of homeostasis, and show gratitude to yourself and your existence.

I.M.S.A.F.E

We pilots have a practice. Every time we choose to fly, we check the latest meteorology reports, assess the plane's condition, and, most importantly, assess the state of a variable considered imperfect, and sometimes even the most faulty cog in the aviation process: ourselves.

I - Illness.

M - Medication.

S - Stress.

A - Alcohol.

F - Fatigue/Food.

E - Emotions/Experience.

The acronym IMSAFE came about as a simple self-evaluation checklist for pilots to determine whether they should remain grounded or fly on a particular day, depending on how they feel. The principle of the practice seems somewhat applicable to everyday life.

Firstly, take care of your physical self. This involves physical activity—going to the gym, yoga, pilates—whatever form of physical activity you enjoy that helps keep you in shape. The more physically put together you are, the better your ability to cope with stress and adversity.

Next, 'medication.' Consult a doctor about any medication you consume; a second opinion never hurts. Know all side effects, and adjust said supplements to your lifestyle, goals, and practices. Aviators also have suitable coping mechanisms to alleviate stress before flight. Following strict checklists to mitigate distractions, constant communication with the tower to remain accountable, meditation or workouts before flights, and many pre-identified stressors assessed before they leave the runway. So why do we not prepare for the daily stress we may face? Developing coping mechanisms will help, like ensuring a daily period of solitude, unwinding, and evaluating our mental well-being to be better prepared for externalities and internalities.

Alcohol and non-medicinal drugs, be they casual, serious, legal, or even illegal, will always have an effect on your emotional state of being. They may be positive in the short term but are always detrimental in the long run, leading to unnatural coercion of your neutral point of homeostasis. They also impair your ability to make logical judgment calls, impede critical awareness, disallow metacognition through the period of intoxication, and you have to cope with the extended detoxification aftereffects. Have fun by all means; some of the wildest stories I laugh about with my friends happened during moments of poor choices and irrational behavior. Make memories; ensure you make them responsibly, and being able to remember them the following day may be a point of consideration.

Food or diet is also a huge factor in health and managing tardiness. What you eat determines how you feel - a terrible diet leads to a dreadful state of mind. Maybe not in your teen years, but I promise you, once you're 23 and devour a whole pizza on your own while binging Ted Lasso, you will feel the aftereffects in the form of meat sweats, bloating, and a food coma. The more balanced your diet, the more balanced your well-being will be. Eventually, you'll start to feel the compounded effects of your (hopefully healthy) eating habits over time.

The last point is probably the most pertinent—your emotional state. There is no shame in grounding yourself, as a pilot or a human being, when you experience emotional discomfort. Your high school breakup is just as valid of an excuse as the death of a loved one. Both of the aforementioned are, believe it or not, just as valid as a simple melancholic day. Only you will know the extent of how much emotional intensity you experience daily, and sometimes it's ok to step back, take a moment for yourself, detach from the world, and come back twice as prepared for the adventure ahead of you.

Aphantasia

When I was in elementary school, the teachers would vividly describe incredible places in the world when they explained historical topics. In middle school, serene landscapes were depicted and visualized in geography. As we grow older, we speak of the good old days, almost like we can see the events unfolding in front of our eyes. You never forget the first time you hold your firstborn child, staring, gazing, lost in your baby's eyes. Widowers, counting the end of their days, speak fondly of the moment they met their dynamite life partner at a run-down bar. I always thought they were speaking metaphorically. I assumed they had a comprehensive acknowledgment of what happened and how they felt, and when imagining the past, they simply told, not actually seeing nor feeling the experience they once lived through. I lived this way for 21 years before I learned the truth.

Aphantasia - "n. the inability to form mental images of objects that are not present."

Aphantasia is a neurological condition in which an individual cannot voluntarily generate images in their mind. This seemed comical, mainly because I was informed that you can even hear, taste, smell, and feel things within the grasp of your mind's eye. Confused and made to feel like I was being pranked, I turned to the internet for answers. Here I came across this:

"Vividness of Visual Imagery Test.

VVIQ Instructions:

For each scenario, try to form a mental picture of the people, objects, or setting. Rate how vivid the image is using the 5-point scale. If you do not have a visual image, rate vividness as '1'. Only use '5' for images that are as lively and vivid as *real seeing*. The rating scale is as follows:

1. No image at all, I only "know" I am think-ing of the object
2. Dim and vague image
3. Moderately realistic and vivid
4. Realistic and reasonably vivid
5. Perfectly realistic, as vivid as real seeing."

Now, try to imagine an apple. A red apple, if you will. Try to visualize the curvature of the body. The evening light glistened on the waxy skin of the perfectly preserved surface of the fruit, branded by a sticker from the local farmers market. Picture the planted stem on the top of the apple: greenish, yet mildly brown, slim at the bottom, and growing in width towards the top. Now, imagine biting into the apple. Your teeth, tearing apart an unaligned wedge, bleeding the sweet liquid within. Can you see the apple? Can you hear the crunch of your teeth piercing through the translucent film of red membrane? Can you taste the tang you've experienced hundreds of times on a Sunday when your parents bought you fruit while you paced around in the dog park?

From the list above, on a scale of 1 - 5, what was the vividness of the image?

Most of you will pick between 2 and 5. However, 3% of the people reading this will see nothing, hear nothing, taste nothing, or visualize nothing. They can comprehend precisely what I describe and connect the dots in their minds, but they will not be able to see. When their eyes are closed, it's pitch black, and there's nothing.

This, by no means, is a mental illness or a lack of cognitive function. The lucky or unlucky few who can't visually imagine are simply hard-wired to think like that. I went 22 years without knowing that I wasn't just imagining things differently from others; I wasn't able to, ever. If you are an aphantasiac, you are probably bad with faces. Maybe you have trouble daydreaming - aphantasiacs can't even dream like everyone else. We see little to no sensory detail. I have been told that dreaming for some is like watching TV or playing a video game from their own point of view. Even more shocking was that they said they visualized memories and dreamt in high definition. As surprising as it may seem, my dreams and memories are comparable to staring at a TV that's been turned off. This changed the way I viewed reality. I was overcome by a feeling of... not inadequacy, but almost as if I couldn't do something magical. To live and then re-live the moment within the confines of your imagination for all of time. Time that is captured in your brain and enjoyed eternally.

This was incredibly frustrating because you can't cure Aphantasia, there's no treatment, and you can't self-learn to visualize with your mind's eye. The only visual experience I will have with my past is the present. And that is a wild realization to have when you are going through an existential crisis in college. I wanted to do something about it, but I could do nothing about it. Being helpless about a situation that you have no control over is one of the most infuriating predicaments life throws at you.

How did I process it? I vowed to live an extraordinary life and absorb every waking moment to its fullest. I chose to document every minor detail that would slip my mind. My friends mocked my pathological need to pull my phone or action camera out at any time to capture a moment from my point of view. I needed to re-create the imagination I lacked, digitally, for me to re-live, capturing the moments that mattered most in their raw and authentic form. This didn't pan out too well for me - which led to my introduction to the hedonic treadmill. A race to experience everything that I could possibly think of. A bucket list that became overwhelmingly lengthy, and a camera roll that grew from a few hundred to a couple of thousands. However, I am grateful for this 'phase' of unapologetically wanting to live a life I am constantly in awe of. It taught me to forget about future consequences and disregard my past, at least briefly.

For almost two years, I lived a ridiculous life of not worrying about money, my future, interviews, grades, and the accouterments that came with the transitionary period from your teenage to an integrated adult of the working populace. For that moment in time, in my own search for purpose, I felt as though I was put on this planet to capture it, to experience the wild twists and turns, the peaks and trenches. I enjoyed documenting and capturing time. I loved creating memories, finding ways to immortalize them in ways that enabled me to re-experience them exactly how they happened: old postcards, the wrapper of a cigar, polaroids that don't facilitate do-overs, b-roll, film, negatives, and mediums that transcend time by simply freezing them. Don't get me wrong; I wasn't trying to be that annoying parent at their child's recital, capturing the performance on their camera rather than being immersed in it. To document moments worthy of being seen as I live and breathe through them gave me an inexplicable level of joy.

The time I spent 'living in the moment' was not just an 'if you feel like it, do it' kind of thing, but rather, an attitude to take pleasure in the miscellaneous task and the exhilarating festivities equally. A focus on the present meant that I was able to enjoy my two to four-mile walk to class in Los Angeles. Instead of seeing it as a repetitive chore, I cherished it. Making coffee in the morning turned into an espresso laboratory with various tools and techniques primed to extract the perfect shot of caffeine. Cramming for exams late into the devil's hour turned into kickbacks with friends, an activity I actively knew was an experience worth being immersed in because sooner or later, when working my nine to five, I'm going to want to be in that odd-smelling study lounge at UCLA with the people who were paramount to the 'visually lacking' memory of the best years of my life.

Our memory is a fickle and complex unit of storage. It's funny because we tend to remember the highlights of the most prominent incidents but forget the whole picture. The beauty of reminiscing is in its imperfections. I have the privilege of reality being whatever I perceive it to be because I don't have a picture-perfect version of it engraved in my head. So when I think about the time my friends and I went skydiving for the first time, we remember the pornstar we ran into in the hangar, the tears of joy, and the portrait of us embracing one another after our feet touched the ground. Still, we forget the uncomfortable 4-hour train journey we made to Diego on three different occasions to make that memory a reality. When I think of my first flight on a single-engine plane,

I forget the tremors and squeals of laughter I underwent the first time I felt a multiplied gravitational force on my limbs, but instead, I remember my first sunset soaring over the Santa Monica pier. I think of the beautiful culture and people I had the pleasure of immersing myself with during my years abroad, but I value the fights and quarrels I had with my roommates equally. I swam with sharks, but I was horribly seasick and threw up on marine life. I've dated women who made me feel like the most important person in the world, but have also been the cause of many insecurities. To have the good, we need the bad. To enjoy ourselves, we need to suffer. Every happy memory is demarcated by the end and the beginning of a sad one. What makes the imperfect memory of your past worth remembering is how well you live your present.

Happiness was never the destination or the goal. Happiness is the journey we take; as comforting or gruesome as that journey may be, it will never lead to self-actualization but will provide you with temporary moments of fulfillment. Your only objective is to be able to collect more positive waves of joy than the mirrored opposite.

"Enjoy the butterflies, enjoy being naive,
enjoy the nerves, the pressure. If you want to
stand on the top from day one, then
there's nothing else to look forward to."
- Daniel Ricciardo.

Time Bank

My high school had a weekly tradition; every Monday morning, the institution's principal would give a speech. It would carry the well-nurtured intent of being inspirational and informative, but unfortunately, it would also, most of the time, put everyone to sleep first thing in the week. One analogy, however, caught my attention and has stuck with me all these years. The story goes like this:

Every day, when the clock strikes 00:00 (midnight), a sum of eighty-six thousand four hundred dollars will be deposited into your bank account. The money will disappear if left in your possession twenty-four hours later. You cannot save it for subsequent use. You cannot transfer it to anyone else. The only way you can utilize it is by spending all the funds every – single – day. The following day, another sum of eighty-six thousand four hundred dollars will be deposited into your bank account, and none will remain from the previous cycle. The catch is that the inflow of money can end without notice, meaning you could wake up one day and have zero dollars in that account.

What would you do? Spend it all? For how long? How much money could you possibly spend on yourself? Would you spend your money on others? Most people would buy anything and everything that they have ever wanted. Some would help their partners, parents, and family members with their newfound wealth. Others would spend it on experiences. You could instead buy jewelry, booze, cars, the simple pleasures. As established before, the money is finite and will stop at any undisclosed time.

What would you do? One thing is certain: you will do everything in your power to spend every last penny, every day.

Now, what if I told you that you have been playing this game your whole life? Only in this instance, you are given eighty-six thousand four hundred seconds of time, instead of eighty-six thousand four hundred units of currency.

For those mourning internally, reassuring themselves that eighty-six thousand four hundred dollars is more valuable than eighty-six thousand four hundred seconds, I offer you a choice: You get 1 billion dollars right now, but the catch is that you won't wake up in the morning. You will not accept money because your life is more valuable than all the money in the world. So when you go to sleep tonight, as your head sinks into the soft pillow, just before you drift away into your vivid dreams, remember that you may not get eighty-six thousand four hundred seconds again. Remember that the final day may come sooner than later, and whatever fleeting seconds you didn't use today are forever lost.

CHAPTER 3

THE PURPLE HEART

The Purple Heart is a medal given to specific individuals who serve in the United States military. It honors heroes who performed above and beyond the call of duty and is a combat decoration presented to all those hurt by instruments of war. By no means is the battlefield equivalent in severity to our day-to-day lives—the brave humans who served are champions of society and harbingers of the sacrifice made in servitude of the noble pursuit to protect.

We fight our battles daily, with significantly smaller stakes, but they are battles nonetheless. We serve to protect the ones we hold dearest to our hearts, be it against outside forces or against ourselves, in an effort to make it to tomorrow. It could even be that we take arms at the front to maintain a stalemate long enough to safeguard our properties, children, friends, and family from all that seek to hurt or destroy our livelihood. We serve through the suffering, the hurt, and the injuries, both physical and emotional alike, for we are caring and compassionate be-ings with primal drivers predicated on social behavior.

The purpose of all living things, according to Darwin, is to reproduce and evolve. Natural selection will then take its course to determine the superior beings capable of survival, or more importantly, procreation. Our rise with-in the natural order as the apex predator of our planet resulted from our conscious ability to protect and outlive divergent species in our ecosystem and increase the fre-quency of generational offspring. The fact of the matter remains: whether we accept it or not, our innate impulse is to sacrifice and fortify our partners and children, even if it were to bring us personal harm.

We may never receive a medal for the love we give or for the sacrifices we make for those who matter to us. We may not fully understand the vulnerability we expose our-selves to by opening up to our friends, family, and loved ones. But we continue to serve, even in the face of poten-tial harm, showing bravery that often goes unrecognized.

This is a long and hard-fought battle. It's you and your troops against the world. You are trusting your life with the people who share the trenches with you, so be very considerate of who you have beside you, fighting back to back for the conflicts and obstacles to come.

Partner in Crime

In an interview conducted by Lex Fridman with Elon Musk, a particular conversation caught my attention:

Fridman: "As the saying goes – 'Be kind, for everyone you meet is fighting a battle you know nothing about.' What is something difficult you are going through that people don't often see?"

Musk: "My mind is a storm. I don't think most people would want to be me. They may think they would want to be me, but they don't. They don't know. They don't understand."

Fridman: "How are you doing?"

Musk: "Overall, ok. In the grand scheme of things, I can't complain."

Fridman: "Do you get lonely?"

Musk: "Sometimes. But I, you know, my kids and friends keep me company."

Fridman: "So not existential?"

Musk: "There are many nights I sleep alone. I don't have to, but I do."

Elon Musk is one of the wealthiest individuals on the planet. He arguably possesses more fame and power than several world leaders and dictators. To the average man, Musk has and can have anything he wants to put his mind to. From a distance, he has it all figured out. But people hide behind facades, an inauthentic show they put on for the public eye, not because they want to - but because they have to. Not everyone wants to understand your struggles; most people don't care, and some don't want to hear your grievances and be reminded of their own. If all the money in the world, space shuttles, cars, media coverage, clothes, and multi-billion dollar companies won't alleviate the loneliness of one of the greatest minds of the 21st century, what would?

The world's oldest study has been tracking thousands of individuals across the globe for over 80 years to understand what factors contribute to their happiness over time. The study began with 268 Harvard undergraduates, including a notable sophomore named John F. Kennedy, who later went on to become the thirty-fifth President of the United States of America. The scientists also tracked the original subjects' immediate family members, including randomized generic pools of biologically unrelated individuals. The progress of the study members was recorded at two-year intervals. Some went on to have successful careers as lawyers, businesspeople, diplomats, and members of high society. Some lived simple lives, the usual nine-to-five, a modest home, a small family, the poster child for the middle-class American dream. There was also a fair sum that retracted in fortune, went bankrupt, became alcoholics, schizophrenics, and a plethora of causes on tracks that weren't inevitable. Everything about these people was recorded: their wins and losses, partners and associates, their emotional affect at different stages of life, and their overall well-being over the specified collection periods.

The head of the study, Robert J. Waldinger, concluded that the result of the most extended study of adult life recorded in the history of humanity points to 'Relationships' as the key to a long, healthy, and happy life. The revelatory discovery was that the researchers found a positive correlation between prosperous relationships and long-term health. Waldinger explained that medical records indicate that a person's social fitness is vital to hindering cognitive and physical deterioration.

The work of Arthur Brooks also led to a similar conclusion. He claims faith, relationships, and 'work that serves other people' are critical proponents of leading a fulfilling life. An important distinction is that faith doesn't necessarily mean 'religious devotion,' although the premise is similar. In this context, faith encompasses your principles and the philosophies that enable you to keep perspective on the radical scale of the construct within which you exist. To be at peace, you will need directives on your path, which is usually influenced heavily by your community and the effects of mimetic theory. "Work that serves other people" is a path for you to find your purpose.

The next chapter will explore this driver in your search for happiness. Relationships, however complicated, are a cornerstone of self-development and self-preservation, acting as a tool for our ultimate purpose, as dictated by natural selection.

> *"Loneliness kills. It's as powerful*
> *as smoking or alcoholism."*
> — *Robert Waldinger.*

The data collected by the study indicated that physical and psychological pain over the span of one's lifetime was significantly lower among those who reported marital satisfaction. Subjects who reported unhappy marriages, divorces, and familial instability experienced physical and mental pain, a more significant effect due to a deficiency in social support. People who showed high levels of social fitness also exhibited restraint to addictive habits such as alcohol intoxication, nicotine dependency, and substance abuse as coping mechanisms to compensate for the lack of emotional support from friends and relatives. The octogenarians were living proof that a stable and secure relationship shielded them from aging as rapidly as others of similar age, alternate circumstances, and reduced mental decline in the latter stages of life.

There we have it. As much as we'd like to believe that "happiness comes from within" and actively work towards critical self-awareness, it is also equally as essential to evaluate your immediate surroundings. I'm sure some people reading this think they are doing great when it comes to acquaintances and family ties because everyone loves them or they have no grievances with other individuals - but as Mike Tyson puts it, 'If you're a friend of everybody, you are an enemy to yourself.'

Aristotle characterizes friendship into three kinds: utility-based, pleasure-based, and character-based friendships. This is self-explanatory: you choose acquaintances based on whether they are helpful, enjoy their company, or value their character. Evaluating your relationships may not be an active consideration process in your day-to-day life; it is a retrospective afterthought for most, but we can group all our relationships into these three categories. For example, a business associate is a friend of utility; you have a mutual understanding of the purpose you each serve in one another's life. It's similar to a 'friends with benefits' type of understanding. However, one person might sometimes engage in a (not so) platonic relationship because they genuinely enjoy the other person's company or character. Unfortunately, this can sometimes be perceived as manipulative behavior or as someone trying to exploit the other person without disclosing their true intentions.

The second is pleasure-based. A 'cheerleader' personality type usually falls in this category. You'd associate
with this person because they are always a good time to
be around, the kind of people you would call to accom-
pany you on a night out. These are the individuals at
your poker nights, the football games, the high school
best friend you occasionally cold call; the pleasure-based
friendship is the call you make when something good
happens. If the only time you find a group of friends interesting is when you get drunk with them, engage in a
bit of gossip, or have particular prerequisites that need
to be fulfilled to value the time spent with a person, then
that, by no means, is a relationship that will last or has
any discernible meaning to you. We falsely perceive that
people with a large group of friends who party, travel,
and have wild experiences are exciting and should be the
benchmark to strive for. The opposite is true; having a
mass selection of acquaintances doesn't necessarily trans-
late to an interesting or meaningful relationship. We may
have quite a few of those individuals in our immediate
vicinity, but they are not adequate substitutions for a
character-based friendship.

A character-based friend is rare. You call this person
when you are at the lowest point of your life. They are the
ones who will sit in the mud with you and provide a shoul-
der for you to cry on. These personalities share significant
compatibility with your temperaments, thought processes,
and reactive behavior. The character-based relationship

is built upon the foundations of trust and understanding, and most often, it has overcome the testament of time. Your life partner should be a character-based relationship and never any of the other options, just as your relationship with your parents or siblings should be. The more of the latter you have in your life, the happier you will be.

The Big Five

Psychologists claim that personality has five core dimensions. D. W. Fiske developed the theory to understand the personalities of different individuals.

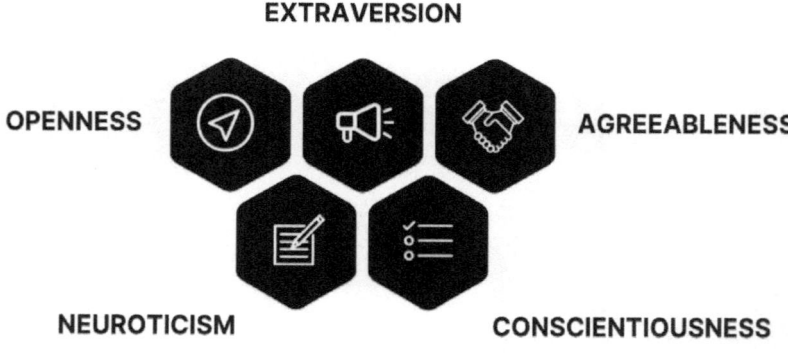

Openness measures one's willingness to learn and explore unfamiliar subjects. It is a measure of creativity and insight in terms of abstract and lateral thought processes. In this context, it would describe a person you could have an open and honest conversation with, with an ability to understand divulging points of view and engage in healthy discourse. People with high levels of openness are intellectually stimulated and excited about trying new things, which keeps life extremely exciting. This is usually the type of friend or partner that orders the most outlandish or extravagant item on the menu, goes on adventures chasing adrenaline, and has an exploratory attitude toward everything. High openness, however, makes it extremely difficult for the people who exhibit the trait to settle into a routine. They crave spontaneity, which requires a lot of flexibility from the people around them due to their reluctance to be lax for anyone but themselves.

Conscientiousness is behavior attributed to low emotional affect and, therefore, shows extreme psychological stability, similar to the 'Judge' discussed in the previous chapter. They don't act on impulse, contrary to a person with high openness, and have a tendency to be reliable and task-oriented, borderline perfectionists. Dependability may sound great in acquaintances, but too much may mean rigidity, resistance to change, and poor collaborative workability. They tend to be the center of conflict not because they attract drama but because their unrealistic standards leave many unresolved issues. The conscientious are the buddies who plan your social trip and create detailed itineraries three months in advance; they are the most stressed and anxious people that you could have around you.

Extraversion embodies social butterflies that thrive in settings that call for interaction and bonding. These people are fun to have around, positive, energetic, and the group's cheerleaders. They ooze positive affect and have

everything figured out, living a blissful life. The 'blissful-
ness' is definitely present in their presence, not because
of their innate capabilities to resolve disputes, but rather
their proficiency in evading unpleasant or threat-resem-
bling aspects in their life. Extraversion tendencies are a
key reason some people may find it nearly impossible to
be alone or rest with their thoughts without constant
distractions and external validation. High extraversion
usually results in attention-seeking behavior through
positive means, but negative too, if the subject is desperate enough. Having a cheerleader around is bearable for
short bursts but isn't sustainable over the long haul.

Agreeableness is a crucial ingredient for satisfaction,
intimacy—emotional and physical—and a strong sense of
security in terms of commitment. These individuals are
empathetic and show emotional literacy, which is
expressed frequently through mutual respect and
supportiveness. This usually makes for good conflict
resolution. There's obviously a caveat: high agreeableness also results in difficulties with confrontation and as-
sertiveness. They may be everyone's support system but
cannot express and process their emotional affect, making
them unhappy or conflicted.

Neuroticism is the 'Mad Scientist,' with high levels
of positive and negative affect that lead them to be hy-
per-aware of emotions, their own and the people around
them, enabling an absence of conflict among associates

due to their ability to resolve quarrels swiftly. Neurotics tend to be sensitive and attuned to relationships; this is comforting because they can build upon interactions through deep and intimate understanding rather than utility and pleasure-based reasons. On the flip side, they show signs of high anxiety and worry, which results in more reactive behavior than someone with high conscientiousness. High neuroticism usually means being an over-thinker, getting in their way within social scenarios and long-term relationships. This, however, also allows them to be careful, curated, machiavellian, and narcissistic due to their talent to avoid conflict, manipulate, and prosper in terms of self-directedness and remuneration.

The reason I have laid out the big five personality traits and their effect on the people around you is because of how they impact your overall well-being. They are the externality that will introduce patterns of scenarios that affect homeostasis. You may have already come to the realization that despite striving to balance all the traits mentioned above within ourselves, we may unfortunately never achieve perfect equilibrium, which is perfectly natural. We will always have more dominant characteristics that influence our personality and choices, so we supplement our deficiencies with those we keep close to ourselves. The most important of these would be your partner.

SONDER

Arthur C Brooks believes that a 'Mad Scientist' should marry a 'Judge,' and a 'cheerleader' should marry a 'Poet.' It is almost ironic that he suggests finding someone who is your complete opposite, possessing traits that you do not, almost as an ode to the saying 'opposites attract.' This is true to a certain extent. Yes, having the cognitive traits you lack in a partner may make a couple the nuclear unit that the world idealizes, but to be high functioning, satisfied, and 'happy,' you need to be somewhat compatible.

Complete opposites may build resentment towards one another due to a clash in lack of excitement from one partner or a scarcity of stability from another. For example, if you are high in openness, consider having a partner or friend who is an academic, explorer, or shares a sense of curiosity. A lack of consciousness will result in conflicts as trivial as daily chores, as with high extraversion comes the difficulties of dating a people-pleaser. Most celebrities struggle with finding partners who are not in similar fields of occupation because they cannot tolerate the extreme levels of extraversion their enterprise requires. The lack of privacy and vertical progress in personal intimacy and concentrations of utility-based relationships will create a void in emotional support.

Agreeableness is almost a prerequisite for people you are close to. If you bicker over your political views, emotional needs, philosophies, and core principles, then there is little to no prospect of forming character-based relationships with this person. Compassion is a derivative of agreeableness, and a lack of it is detrimental to any relationship. Neuroticism is pertinent in a partner because a person unable to comprehend or accept contrary points of view and emotions won't ever be able to handle the ups and downs of a relationship.

The key is to surround yourself with individuals who balance your personality traits. They almost dampen our quirks and self-destructive tendencies, and vice versa. By actively prioritizing compatibility with the third-party externalities that influence your actions daily, you will be able to form a substantially more significant number of character-based friendships.

The Contagion

The Framingham Heart Study is a renowned longitudinal study that has been ongoing since 1948, involving thousands of participants and yielding numerous insights into the causes of heart disease and other health conditions. One of the most notable studies conducted as part of the Framingham Heart Study explored whether happiness is contagious and can spread from person to person within social networks. The study was conducted over a period of 20 years and yielded fascinating insights into the dynamics within societies.

The study followed over four thousand individuals from 1983 to 2003 and measured their happiness using a validated four-item scale. The researchers found that clusters of happy and unhappy people were visible in the network, and the relationship between people's emotions extended up to three degrees of separation. This means that a person's emotional state can be influenced by the feelings expressed by a friends' friends' friend. The research revealed that people surrounded by many happy people and those central in the network are more likely to become satisfied in the future. The researchers used longitudinal statistical models to show that clusters of happiness result from the spread of joy rather than just people associating with similar individuals. The study also found that the impact of happiness decayed over time and with geographical separation. Based on these findings, the examination concludes that a person's happiness is influenced by the happiness of those they are connected to. This supports the idea that happiness, like health, is a collective phenomenon.

Further analysis suggests that mimicking other people's actions, whether for a few seconds or several weeks, can impact the emotional state of the copied individuals. This influence can be observed in the shortest interactions, such as a passerby's smile or nod. It shows that even the briefest of interactions can affect our mood in the short term, leading one to consider how our family, social circles, and even the effects of third-party individuals with whom we may not come into close contact can impact our overall well-being.

Your happiness can be affected up to the three degrees of separation. Unknown individuals interacting with the people you associate with can alter your emotional affect. It lends to reason that your environment is not mutually exclusive to your 'happiness' but is a crucial determinant of your overall emotional experience. This, of course, means that a cluster of individuals with a majority that shares a sense of heightened happiness will be able to transfer that to the community surrounding them.

Similarly, a crowd of miserable interactions will spread adverse effects through your immediate surroundings and then transfer over to subsequent interactions.

So run away from misery. Detach yourself not only from the depressed, the unlucky, and the chronically problematic but also from the unpleasant because even a handshake, the tone of a voice, or repeated interaction with the unwelcome will give you the bug. This isn't avoidance-fueled behavior; this is self-preservation. You can cut off friends, even terminate relationships with partners, fire lazy employees, or move to a different country, but you are stuck with your family for life, for better or worse. You can't replace your parents, relatives, children, or siblings. No matter how hard and unhealthy interacting with them may be. It could benefit all parties involved if you inject a degree of positivity into a dysfunctional system. It may never solve the problem, but it can potentially improve your quality of life. You equally have an effect on others, just as they do. Unfortunately, if you are part of the overwhelming minority, no matter your efforts, the result will always be misery.

Now, begin to evaluate your surroundings. Consider the type of people you engage with. Review the qualities of personalities that would bring you the greatest satisfaction and fulfillment in your life. Don't just stop there. Extend your awareness beyond your inner circle to the outermost layers of social interferences to maximize or minimize your exposure to the reciprocal effects.

"We are the average of the five people
we spend the most time with."
- Jim Rohn.

The quote pertains to the law of averages, *"n. the principle that supposes most future events are likely to balance any past deviation from a presumed average."* Put simply, it means that the frequency of occurrences will correspond to its probability. Like it or not, we are creatures that are victims of influence, and we cannot deny it. Consequently, controlling the type and degree to which we allow subjection to said influence is paramount. Why not surround yourself with the necessary qualities, attributes, support, and encouragement? Why not mimic what you hope to become in the utopian future you envision for yourself? The quality of the five people you are closest to must result in what you strive for, and anything short of this will lead to the inevitable: dissatisfaction with the person you become.

A purple heart is inevitable. The bruises, losses, and sacrifices you make in battle and in service to the individuals you care for are a mark of noble existence. Find comrades fit to fight alongside you, friends, colleagues, and partners whom you would go to battle with, to find strength and solace in one another despite the relentless adversity endured. The people you share that suffering with will determine the legacy you leave behind.

PART TWO

INTROSPECTION

CHAPTER 4

A HIERARCHY OF NEEDS

While watching a movie, I heard an actor say "I feel complete," during a joyous moment. The actor played the role of a mother with one child who lived comfortably in a supportive family environment, was in a secure relationship, and had a stable job. Of course, life can be a self-fulfilling prophecy leading to a happy or not-so-happy ending when crafted by creatives in a writer's room. But is it possible to achieve a sense of completion and satisfaction in real life? Can we ever be content with our state of being if we are besieged by the avalanche of problems that life throws at us? If not an endless cavalcade of obstacles, then perhaps the chronic fear of imminent threats that may never materialize. By the way, the character from the movie, the one I mentioned at the start of the paragraph, was unexpectedly shot and killed within the next five minutes of the film.

It turns out that problems and suffering can be beneficial, but they do not necessarily affect our overall satisfaction in life. In the early 20th century, Abraham Maslow published his theory of the 'Hierarchy of Needs.' I first learned about this theory as a means to motivate employees in the corporate world, understanding what a leader needs to provide their subordinates for them to become high-functioning members of an organization. However, the scope of the theory extends far beyond the workplace, and here's how:

Maslow's Hierarchy of Needs

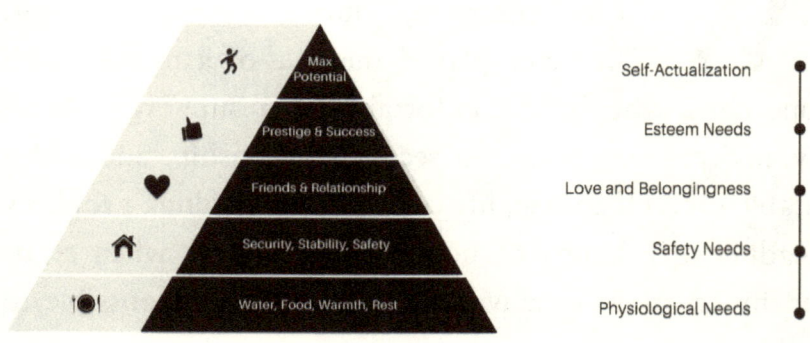

While the world was focused on correcting behavioral complications in the office, humanists, such as Maslow, believed that all people conduct themselves in a manner that achieves a particular goal.

n. "Humanism is a philosophical stance that emphasizes the potential and agency of human beings, both individually and socially. It considers them the starting point for serious intellectual and moral inquiry".

A stack of evolving needs and wants that ultimately lead to self-actualization.

Self-actualization: *n.* *"the realization or fulfillment of one's talents and potentialities, especially considered as a drive or need present in everyone."*

Self-actualization is often thought of as the ultimate goal in life, where one will supposedly experience perpetual happiness. It is seen as the point where all echelons have been completed, all achievements unlocked, and the final bosses defeated - Mario beating Bowser or Thanos losing to Stark. However, the reality is that self-actualization isn't a checkbox that can be ticked off, guaranteeing a "happily ever after." Instead, it is a process - a continuous journey of self-improvement and self-fulfillment. It's not a destination but rather a lifelong path toward personal growth. While you may never fully achieve it, you will always move towards it, one step at a time.

Like anything, solving problems requires working through stages to find solutions. Arthur C. Brooks claimed that satisfaction, purpose, and enjoyment are three key factors that contribute to happiness. Maslow portrays five stages of motivation, each built upon the other, that pave the road to self-actualization, aligning with psychologists' interpretation of happiness and fulfillment.

The two foundation levels of the hierarchy of needs are 'Basic Needs,' encompassing physiological and safety requirements. The most fundamental of these is physiological, which comprises all necessary conditions to meet the primal needs of survival and reproduction. This can range from food, water, shelter, sexual reproduction, air for breathing, and even homeostasis - basic human necessities that address the most rudimentary intuitions and desires, enabling individuals to evolve beyond needs to wants.

After satisfying physiological needs, one's safety and security needs must be met. This could include financial security and insurance against potential threats and damages, not only to property but also to oneself and their loved ones. Ensuring these needs are met secures one's physiological needs and alleviates worry and anxiety about future threats. The state and its citizens have a preexisting social contract that ensures the protection of rights through the justice system and other law enforcement agencies. Financial institutions offer monetary support, such as savings and lines of credit, to meet these security needs. Your occupation, retirement funds, and even unemployment benefits play a significant role in fulfilling safety/security needs. It is important to note that the next stage of the hierarchy will only be viable for an individual if their basic safety needs are met.

After basic needs are met, humans are confronted with psychological needs: Social and Esteem Needs. Social Needs can be anything that counters loneliness. The World Health Organization has recognized social isolation as a "priority public health problem." To further add to the credibility of this epidemic, the Surgeon General of the United States of America claims that the damaging effects of loneliness are equivalent to smoking fifteen cigarettes a day. To satisfy social needs, one must feel a sense of belonging, love, affection, and, most importantly, acceptance.

This is usually achieved through romantic relationships, familial ties, meaningful friendships, and a community. A key prong of happiness is enjoyment; you need a social support system to have that facet of life. Most people believe in god, some show relentless support to their local sports team, and others spend their whole weekend in the country club. You could assume that these people have given high priority to God, games, and even posh environments, but we fail to acknowledge that all the activities above foster cooperative communities. Religion tends to be a support system for many, giving them purpose and meaning in their struggles. Sports indiscriminately creates a common purpose for large groups of people to unite in agreement on a shared struggle. A country club is a convention for like-minded individuals from unrelatable walks of life, curating a community for themselves to expunge loneliness. We all require a medium to express our social cravings, and being left unfulfilled will result in a sense of incomplete existence.

Esteem Needs, on the tier above Social Needs, are a set of requirements reserved for those with an abundance of physiological, safety, and social injections into their livelihood. When the fundamental and foundational tiers of social acceptance are fulfilled, individuals tend to pursue respect and appreciation. In this stage, prestige, ego, and recognition for accomplishments are core contributors to motivation. Individuals seek or identify purpose at this level; schooling, honors, awards, workplace promotions, monetary remuneration, and fame are all weighed to measure personal worth. This can only be achieved through the perception that your contribution to the world is valued by a third party. This fosters self-esteem and confidence as a direct result of vertical achievement. Conversely, a lack of self-esteem or an inflated want for recognition with deficiencies in the lower levels of the pyramid of hierarchy would result in insecurity, feeling inferior, or resulting in the development of imposter syndrome.

Imposter Syndrome

n. "the persistent inability to believe that one's success is deserved or has been legitimately achieved as a result of one's own efforts or skills."

A monologue by Larry Summers, former President of Harvard University, stated on a panel at the All-In Summit, "We have gone from thinking that self-esteem comes from achievement to thinking that achievement comes from self-esteem. Am I worried about that? Yeah, I absolutely am. Am I worried about the finances? Am I worried about our inadequate investment in technology and leadership? Am I worried about a kind of broad constipation? Many of you have probably been to Harvard Square. There's a bridge. The bridge goes over the Charles River. It's 362 feet long. It had been around for 100 years. It needed to be fixed. 62 months. It took five years and two months, with one lane of traffic closed, to renovate a 362-foot bridge. To put that in perspective, G. S. Patton built a bridge over the Rhine, 3000 feet, in one day. I wandered over to the classics department one day and learned that Julius Caesar built his bridge Over The Rhine, 3000 feet, not 300 feet, in nine days. And this is what it took us. So, do we have huge problems? Yes. Is this the first time we've had huge problems? Hell no. Is there a prospect that we can solve those problems? Yes, I think there is. Do I think we, all things considered, have a more solvable set of problems and a more dynamic society for solving them? Yeah, I do."

Before the cultural changes of the 21st century, humanity looked to external validation and achievements to build self-esteem. Our sense of self-worth was a product of accomplishments and accolades. Shifting paradigms of our understanding of self-worth suggest that self-esteem is now seen as a foundation for achievement. A strong sense of self-worth is a great motivator to set incredibly ambitious goals. We continue pursuing unattainable, unrealistic goals despite setbacks due to inflated self-esteem. Imposter syndrome is sometimes the realization of incompetence, maybe warranted or not, due to the increase in self-esteem in the masses without the necessary time, struggles, and collection of pertinent skills and emotional control that fosters competence. This furthers our anxiety and depression due to our fears of being ousted as lacking proficiency, leading to self-destructive behavior.

Your belief that you are a gift to society is a delusion without a trail of specific (S), measurable (M), achievable (A), and timely (T) hurdles that have been crossed. This is known as the S.M.A.R.T. criteria for defining goals: a concept that allows individuals to be realistic about their ambitions.

Body dysmorphia, for example, is not exclusively caused by constant comparison of yourself to others but also because of self-esteem that has been built paradoxically. A writer may feel inadequate because he/she may not have written or read sufficient content in the past. An athlete may feel anxious about a race, especially if they had poor practice or have never experienced losing. This can also reduce the positive impact of winning and the lessons that come with it. Similarly, anxiety may arise if you lack the expertise required for a task and fear being exposed. The solution is simple—focus on personal growth and measurable achievements instead of trying to fill a void with an unearned sense of entitlement. This will help you gain self-esteem, a sense of belonging, security, and fulfillment of your physiological needs.

Self-actualization = Physiological Needs + Safety Needs + Social Needs + Esteem Needs.

At the very peak of Masalow's Hierarchy of Needs is a metacognitive being. Self-actualizing individuals are self-aware, driven by purpose and a constant pursuit of self-improvement; they are not exclusively rich in wealth but also rich in mind. Their sense of self-worth stems from within, building immunity to external validation. They seek to exploit their potential by harnessing the total capacity of achievable Satisfaction, Purpose, and Enjoyment. Ultimately, they bridge the space between themselves and happiness.

The Disciplined Mind

"Discipline is the highest form of self-love"
- Rafael Rolli.

The word 'discipline' carries an inherently negative connotation, as one would not often associate positive feelings towards it. 'Discipline' is viewed to be difficult or opposite to the feeling of wanting. How is it self-love? This will not be the usual spiel about delaying instant gratification for long-term gain. The reality of the quote is quite contrary. Discipline is your ability to face and manage adversity. It is the art of suffering towards striving for a state of satisfaction. Discipline is your ability to enjoy the struggles and savor the fruits of your labor instead of mourning the bitter aftertaste of regret. We have established that the moment of achievement after long-term struggles or short-term comfort in the form of dopamine-based gratification is short-lived. Having the discipline to formulate a biological want-management strategy is self-love. Discipline is wanting less, inherently leaving you delighted with everything you have. Enjoyment, too, requires a level of discipline to control your rate of exposure to the pleasure of company and other joys before the effects of diminishing marginal utility take over. Discipline gives you mastery over emotions and impulses, fostering mental fortitude.

Modern society understands the importance of physical reps in the gym, the occasional 5k run, and the 'healthy body - healthy mind' attitude. Like any other muscle in our body, our brain receives repertory conditioning based on our thoughts and bodily reactions. Like any muscle, constant training and supplementary input will inevitably result in the desired outcome. It's entirely possible that we don't consider our brains to function this way, so we neglect it.

Our minds constantly evolve and adapt, shaping themselves through the experiences we accumulate. Recent studies in neuroscience research suggest that this process continues well into our mid-twenties. The habits we cultivate during these formative periods profoundly impact our cognitive abilities later in life. Just like a sponge, our brains absorb and retain conditioning, information, and skills, both beneficial and detrimental, a malleability that makes us susceptible to the illusory truth effect.

Illusory Truth Effect: *n. "The illusory truth effect is the tendency to believe false information after it has been repeated often enough."*

Imagine a lie you've told, one you've repeated countless times. You've honed your delivery, imbuing it with a convincing air of authenticity. Initially, you may be aware of the deception, but as time passes, the sharpness of recollection fades, the details blur, and the fabricated narrative becomes your truth. The line between fact and falsehood becomes indistinguishable.

The illusory truth effect is a cognitive bias affecting how we process information. When we encounter information repeatedly, our brains process it more efficiently, creating a sense of familiarity and trustworthiness. This can lead us to believe that the information is accurate, even if it's false. The more we hear something, the more likely we are to accept it as fact. This phenomenon has important implications, especially in advertising, politics, and the spread of misinformation. Advertisers use the illusory truth effect to make their claims more persuasive, while politicians use it to influence public opinion.

When we repeatedly engage in negative thoughts, habits, or behaviors that prevent us from achieving our goals, we reinforce our tendency to avoid those goals. For example, if you make a commitment to exercising every day but consistently skip your workouts, you train your brain to accept this behavior as normal. Unfortunately, this can lead to a subconscious pattern of avoidance that makes it even harder to maintain discipline over time.

Individuals who quit cigarettes or sugar exhibit a similar pattern of behavior. Initially, they experience a surge of dopamine due to short-term success. However, with time, it becomes increasingly challenging to maintain disciplined adherence to the commitment, leading to a loss of interest. Eventually, a cheat day is allowed, or a problematic circumstance forces the individual to rekindle the habit. While the initial guilt may be overwhelming, they adapt to the discomfort with repetition, gradually losing control over their behavior altogether. As a result, the cycle resets, and they must then painstakingly recover all the progress that has now been lost.

The Habit Loop

James Clear refers to the four laws of 'Behaviour Change' in his hit novel 'Atomic Habits.' The first of the four laws is to create an environment with visible and obvious cues that repetitively remind you to perform a desired action. The more prominent a task is, the more likely you are to complete it. Take your toothbrush, for example; the first thing you see on your bathroom counter is probably a brightly colored toothbrush and toothpaste, which will then act as a physical stimulus to perform tasks such as brushing your teeth but also lead to subsequent habits such as flossing and using your mouthwash. Other visual cues, perhaps the form of a gym outfit, can motivate you towards healthier habits like getting a daily run-in.

The Second Law is to make a habit appealing. This is the basis of the concept. By making a habit enjoyable, you inherently develop a sense of gratification upon its completion, thus leading you to maintain consistency in performance. For instance, I hate reading, particularly fiction, which, to me, is one of the most boring things I could hope to do with my time. Alternatively, I enjoy business-related content, technology, finance, and even psychology, so reading in the form of business magazines, like the Wall Street Journal, was always fascinating.

"Find a job you love, and you will never
have to work a day in your life"
- Mark Twain.

Another instance that comes to mind is a time when I disliked some of my high school classes. When I got to college, however, I had the freedom to choose courses that genuinely interested me. As a result, education became less of a chore and more of an enjoyable act of self-improvement. This is a perfect example of how the theory can be applied to reality.

The third law is to first make a habit easy, then gradually increase the total effort you input over time to acclimatize towards the overall objective. Bodybuilders and powerlifters utilize a technique known as progressive overload when exercising their muscles. When attempting to lift a substantial amount of weight, they don't immediately load up to 1000 pounds, as they may break a bone or two while losing consciousness. Instead, they begin with a light and manageable weight, loading gradually and incrementally over a specified period, creating points of personal records before ever attempting the maximum weight.

Similarly, your habits must be achieved methodically: First, do the bare minimum, and only then should you begin to add resistance. The '5 AM Club' is a reference to individuals who wake up at the time mentioned above to get a headstart on their day. This phenomenon is usually associated with highly successful individuals such as CEOs and billionaires.

If you typically wake at 11:30 AM after a pub crawl, tailgate, Netflix marathon, or whatever you do into the early hours of borrowed time from the following day, you won't be able to join the 5 AM Club initially. Even if you persevere and wake up at that time for a few days, the habit is not sustainable in the long run; your routine will simply reject the effort by shutting your body down for the remainder of the day. However, you could attempt to wake up at 10:30 AM and then 9:30 AM, maybe try 8 AM or 6 AM... if you're already at 6 AM, from there onwards, 5 AM becomes very achievable. Making tasks easy will enable you to adhere to them religiously.

The final law is to reward yourself for your suffering. In other words, make a habit or task as satisfying as possible. Think of the times when you sat at the dinner table and your mom told you you couldn't have dessert before you finished your vegetables—the effect of receiving dessert as a reward is similar. Finish work, and you can go home. Get through your workout, and you can have a guilt-free cheat meal. Finish a task on your checklist and enjoy crossing it off a piece of paper. The satisfying feeling of running a pencil line through a task can fill you with as much dopamine as the auditory cue of a text message. The psychology is similar. The sound you hear from the speakers of your phone when you receive a text message causes a spike in dopamine, encouraging you to pick it up. The theme song of any TV show invokes excitement in you before the beginning of the storyline, priming you and signaling you to prepare with a weighted blanket, popcorn, or a refreshing beer. These are all rewards and cues that trigger a sense of compensation in the form of instant gratification in your psyche. Creating rewards for healthy habits is another form of metacognition that enables you to perform at your optimum levels.

THE HABIT LOOP

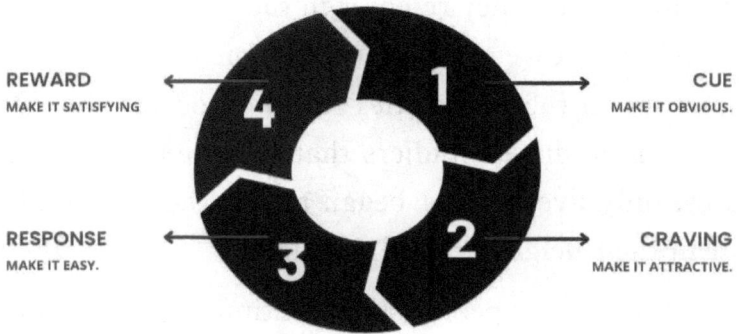

The Habit Loop is a four-step process that allows any individual to break poor habits and cultivate good ones instead. The four laws—make it obvious, make it attractive, make it easy, and make it satisfying—all contain a crucial element that makes a habit adoptable.

One of the abovementioned elements is 'Cues' and 'Triggers'. Visual cues like a toothbrush or workout clothes send signals to the brain, motivating a behavior. This could be a place, a person, or even a word. In 1971, twenty percent of soldiers of the United States armed forces stationed in Vietnam had developed an addiction to heroin. Almost thirty-five percent had at least tried the potent narcotic. This caused widespread panic in the political chambers of Washington D.C., prompting the creation of the Special Action Office of Drug Abuse Prevention. The office, under the Nixon administration, was responsible for the rehabilitation of soldiers and the prevention of narcotics dependency among veterans and the communities they re-enter in the Western world. The researchers, however, presented results that were contradictory to the authorities' bleak expectations. Of all the heroin-addicted soldiers that returned to the United States, only five percent began to use the drug within a year in their neighborhood of origin.

Out of the five percent that continued the use of heroin, eighty-two percent were successfully rehabilitated and did not report a relapse three years after being discharged from the rehab centers. These findings were astonishing! How did nine out of ten soldiers addicted to heroin overcome their habit overnight? Keeping in mind that heroin is one of the most potent and addictive drugs known to man, it is considered to be a permanently obsessional substance.

The spontaneous dissolution in their pattern of behavior came due to a shift in environment, completely eliminating all cues that promoted heroin use. The soldiers were not bombarded by the stressors of war in their homes. They were also not surrounded by other soldiers, addicted to a substance that provided an escape from their mutual suffering. The physical separation of all cues and the re-introduction of healthy relationships enabled the soldiers to eliminate their habits unconsciously. This is textbook behavior observed in drug users. People with an addiction are usually sent to rehabilitation centers, away from friends and an environment that provides them potentially triggering cues and access to promote drug-abusive behaviors. They get clean in a new place, then relapse after returning due to exposure to all the triggers that didn't exist during their recovery.

You need to be aware of your social and environmental cues to break bad habits or cultivate new healthy alternatives. These triggers will determine how much control you possess over your actions. Mastery over one's habits is vital to managing desires, needs, and wants.

Routine, structure, and impulse control are critical to achieving homeostasis.

Cravings and Desires are other integral factors one must combat to uphold habits. Temptation bundling is a technique used to pair pleasure-providing indulgences with behaviors that provide delayed rewards; I call this the 'avocado brownie.' Jokes aside, this technique partially satisfies desires but incorporates elements of healthy habits, such as watching your favorite TV show while running on the treadmill. One company that has utilized this technique in the modern market is Peloton, an aerobic exercise machine manufacturer who has used this approach to sell millions of dollars of products to individuals who may or may not have enjoyed static exercises.

Peloton did this by adding a large interactive display on their equipment, enabling individuals to share workout details and compete with one another. This added a social element to an activity that most people detest: cardio. I listen to entertaining podcasts when hitting legs in the gym, and in this way, I combat my insecurities about being shaped like an inverted triangle.

The final factor that helps build a strong habit is the act itself and the reinforcement of said action in the form of rewards. This, of course, could be done by rewarding yourself with things you enjoy, but the key to performing any habit is to remain consistent for 66-88 days. No, not 21 days; that's a myth. A habit takes two to eight months to become an unconscious routine. For example, if we feel unhygienic, we automatically want to shower, just like you want to brush your teeth in the morning. A shower used to be considered an unpleasant chore in the Victorian era. Children still hate taking showers. You performed these tasks consistently for years before they became second nature, eventually becoming a reward in itself. Doing a task for an extended period of time, as opposed to a short one, is more likely to integrate it into an ingrained part of your life, thus removing the element of gratification needed to complete it.

However, those who need extra help might try habit stacking, which follows the theory that a pattern of multiple habits is easier to follow than a singular outlier in your routine. For example, if you want to start using a new face cream, add it to your schedule in tandem with a strong habit. Using the face cream just before you sleep and leaving it by your bedside table will help integrate the habit as a visual cue and add sleep as a reward for applying the cream.

We are all actors on the stage of our environment, navigating the backdrop and props that influence our every thought and action. This stage, however, can be redesigned and transformed from a place of struggle to a haven of self-improvement through understanding the power of cue elimination, reward reversal, and identity change, through which we can become the architects of our lives, crafting a space that fosters our growth and un-locks our true potential.

Imagine a cluttered room overflowing with unhealthy snacks and objects used in performing health-risking be-haviors. Seeing these objects triggers unwanted manners, making resisting temptation and pursuing healthy habits difficult. This is the power of cues, the unconscious trig-gers that shape our choices without us even realizing it. We must eliminate these negative cues to overcome this, decluttering our physical and mental spaces to create a clear path toward our goals.

Eliminating cues is only the first step, however. We must also rewire our reward system, shifting the focus from immediate gratification to the intrinsic satisfaction that comes from achieving our goals. Instead of reaching for that sugary snack, we can celebrate small wins with activities we genuinely enjoy, associating pleasure with positive behaviors. This reward reversal rewires our brain, making healthy choices feel inherently rewarding.

The final piece of the puzzle is identity change. When we see ourselves as capable and deserving of success, we naturally make choices that align with our desired image. Affirmations, visualizations, and surrounding ourselves with positive role models can help us cultivate a new self-image that fuels our motivation and propels us to-ward our goals. These three principles: cue elimination, reward reversal, and identity change – work together to create a powerful force for self-improvement. By designing an environment that supports our desired behaviors, we can overcome obstacles, break free from negative patterns, and unlock our full potential.

This power extends beyond individual transformation. By carefully designing workplaces, schools, and communities, we can create environments that promote health, well-being, and prosocial behavior, creating a ripple effect that leads to a more positive and sustainable future.

The journey of environmental design starts with self-awareness. Reflect on your current environment and identify the areas hindering your progress. Once you have a clear understanding, implement environmental design principles to create the stage that sets you up for success. Remember, change takes time and effort. Be patient, celebrate your progress, and don't be afraid to experiment to find what works best for you.

Aimless Anxiety

"Frightened of my futureless life,
scared by my foolish anxieties,
unable to see ahead and aiming nowhere,
I continued ceaselessly living
my ridiculously idiotic life."
-Tatsuhiko Takimoto.

Imagine being adrift on an endless ocean, where the vastness is overwhelming, and the direction is uncertain. This feeling of aimlessness can be a breeding ground for anxiety, where the days blur together, and the future feels unmoored. Just as a ship without a rudder is tossed about by the waves, our minds become restless and filled with anxieties when lacking a sense of purpose.

Abraham Maslow placed self-actualization, the desire to reach our full potential, at the pinnacle of human needs. It should be no surprise that this innate drive to find meaning and purpose creates a powerful current in our lives. When we feel stagnant, adrift in a sea of unfulfilled dreams, we feel like the sails of our ship lying limp, unable to catch the wind of possibility.

Psychologist Martin Seligman, who is a pioneer in the field of positive psychology, studied the idea of "learned helplessness," a phenomenon where people who feel like they have no control over their lives start to feel powerless and hopeless. They find it challenging to resolve difficult situations, leading to a pattern of exposure to which they become acclimatized. This state of being can make it challenging to detach themselves from their situation, even when presented with a solution or escape. Instead, they prefer to remain in their unfavorable state of life, constantly complaining and expressing high levels of dissatisfaction with their choices.

The theory of learned helplessness was accidentally discovered during experiments on dogs, where the researchers exposed the canines to inescapable bursts of electricity using an electric shock collar. Over time, the dogs stopped trying to avoid the electric shocks and accepted them as an inevitable part of their existence. The researchers then replaced the hounds with humans and the electric collar with loud noises.

The subsequent human trials concluded that most subjects failed to take any action to mitigate the startling sound after they were unable to prevent it during the initial trial. Even though they were presented with options to escape the stimulant in the trials that followed, they still did nothing. Martin Seligman and Steven Maier discovered that repeated trauma and failure to escape it trained the psychology of the victims to become help-less, corroding away their locus of control and their level of self-efficacy.

Locus of Control:

"Internal locus of control refers to the belief that an individual has personal control over their behavior and life. This means that control comes from within, and those with an internal locus of control tend to have a higher sense of personal agency and self-efficacy. In other words, they believe that they have the power to influence and shape their lives according to their own choices and actions."

Self Efficacy:

"Self-efficacy is a psychological concept that refers to an individual's belief in their ability to achieve specific goals. It reflects a person's confidence in their capacity to control their motivation, behavior, and social environment. These self-evaluations can affect various aspects of human experience, such as the goals people set, the effort they put in to achieve those goals, and the likelihood of reaching a certain level of performance."

It is important to recognize the two internal aspects of your psyche that play a critical role in maintaining your confidence in your ability to overcome the challenges of daily life and in empowering yourself. Learned helplessness also creates a false belief that you are incapable of dealing with the difficulties you face, causing you to become trapped and unable to find a way out. Have you ever faced a difficult situation that seemed insurmountable? How you explain or interpret this situation to yourself can either motivate you to move forward or paralyze you with fear. This ability to interpret events is known as your "attribution style," and it can greatly impact your tendency to feel helpless in the face of adversity.

Learned helplessness can also be considered a mental cage resulting from repeated defeats and negative self-talk. Inside this cage, challenges seem unconquerable; effort feels futile, and motivation crumbles. When someone faces a tough time in life, a pessimistic outlook might make them believe that bad things happen to them because they are unlucky, incompetent, or unworthy and that nothing they can do can change that. This is similar to the classic experiment where dogs, unable to escape shocks, became passively resigned; both exemplifying learned helplessness. Any unpleasant incident or experience reaffirms this negativity, reinforces the cage, and weakens self-belief and the will to try. An optimistic outlook would suggest that while bad things do happen, one can both learn from them and improve their reaction to them. This aligns with the power of self-efficacy, which is emphasized in social cognitive theory. Even after experiencing disappointment, optimism fosters growth, builds resilience, and strengthens self-belief. People who struggle with depression or anxiety often find themselves trapped in pessimistic thinking.

It's important to remember that your attribution style acts like a mental filter, coloring your perception of challenges. By embracing optimism, you can break free from the cage of learned helplessness and develop the resilience to overcome life's obstacles. Feeling adrift, with no control over the direction of your life, can trigger the amygdala, your brain's fear center, leading to a cascade of anxiety. It has been found through research that our minds tend to be most unhappy when we let them wander aimlessly and start ruminating on past mistakes or worrying about an uncertain future. This is similar to a sailor stuck below deck, unable to see the horizon, becoming consumed by fear and doubt. In the same way, our anxieties tend to grow when we lose sight of our goals and purpose.

However, just as a sailor can find solace in the camaraderie of their crew, humans also have a fundamental need for connection and belonging. The desire for interpersonal attachments is an essential human motivation. Feeling isolated and disconnected from others can further exacerbate the anxieties that arise from aimlessness. Just as a ship without a crew would struggle to navigate the vast ocean, we need the support and encouragement of others to find our way through turbulent times.

The journey to find our anchor, that guiding light that provides direction and meaning, is a profoundly personal one. It requires introspection, experimentation, and a willingness to examine uncharted territories of your mind. For some, this anchor may be found in setting personal goals and charting a course toward their dreams and aspirations. For others, it may lie in pursuing meaningful activities and contributing their talents and skills to something larger than themselves. Most find solace in fostering deep connections with loved ones and building a support system that provides strength and resilience.

The key is to uncover goals that align with our core values and interests. Just as a ship needs a rudder that aligns with its hull, our goals must be compatible with our inner compass, allowing us to navigate the seas with confidence, akin to the Mark Twain quote from earlier: "Find a job you enjoy doing, and you will never have to work a day in your life," a fact that science has found to be true.

Discovering your anchor can be challenging, and there will be moments when the conditions become stormy, and the winds of uncertainty blow forcefully. However, just like an experienced sailor can learn to navigate through the roughest of storms, you, too, can learn to overcome your anxieties and find your way to a peaceful state of mind.

Man's Search for Meaning

Most self-help gurus peddle sunshine and rainbows, promising happiness like free samples at your nearest Costco. The path to discovering your 'glorious purpose,' however, may not be about finding a fixed destiny but about embracing the inherent uncertainty of existence and actively choosing a path that aligns with your values and aspirations. Whether that path leads to grand acts or smaller moments of connection and growth, the 'glorious' aspect rises from the conscious creation of your own meaning and purpose.

Viktor Frankl saw some real darkness in his pursuit to understand human motivation; concentration camps and Nazi salute-in-your-face types of darkness. And guess what? He didn't just survive, he grew. Not because he visualized puppies or chanted "good vibes only," but because he found meaning and purpose through adversity, the kind that punches suffering in the face and says, "Not today, Satan." This story, by no means, is a justification or silver lining for all the injustice and atrocities of the period. Instead, it is a reassuring sentiment that even in the darkest days, there is hope.

Frankl was a doctor, treating Viennese folks with their neurosis and existential angst. Then the Nazis showed up, turning his world into what was quite literally purgatory. He ended up in a camp, stripped of everything, facing daily threats of death. Most folks would crumble, right? They become shells of their former selves, begging for the sweet escape of oblivion.

But not Frankl. He observed phenomena within the confines of the camps in the prisoners, something others didn't. He saw that even in the face of unimaginable suffering, even when life throws you enough shit to fill a landfill, there was still a flicker of hope that was held onto. Unlike many who succumbed to the effects of learned helplessness and began to accept their inevitable fate, some found solace even in shackles. It could be in the love they shared with one another, the act of helping someone else in their collective suffering, the beauty of a sunset over barbed wire, or the holy scriptures they devoted themselves to. This wasn't some airy-fairy hope; it was the kind that says, "I may not control what happens to me, but I control how I respond."

These observations formed the basis of logotherapy, his theory that the primary human motivation was the search for meaning, even in the most extreme of circumstances. He said you must stare the abyss in the face and choose meaning, even if it means finding beauty in a pile of dung (which, let's be honest, is a pretty impressive feat).

Frankl believed that even when deprived of everything humane, the mortal spirit retains the ability to discover purpose. By no means is the good doctor encouraging you to ignore your pain; it's about using it as fuel to find your purpose, your "why" in the midst of "what the hell."

So, the next time you're feeling like life's kicked you in the teeth, remember Frankl. Remember that even in the worst situations, there's meaning and motivation to be found. It might not be the pot of gold at the end of the rainbow, but it's something, and that something can make all the difference.

CHAPTER 5

GLORIOUS PURPOSE

Worth World War II ended on the 2nd of September 1945, when the Japanese officially surrendered to President Truman's government of the United States of America. However, the fighting persisted until the 9th of March 1974, almost 30 years after the absolute submission of the imperial forces — one dead man carried on the fight. Lieutenant Hiroo Onoda, declared dead in 1959, was stationed on a tiny island called Lubang within the territory of the Philippines during the concluding phases of the war. Onoda was ordered to hold the island at all costs, waiting for the imperial army to relieve him of his duty. He was to never falter in the face of adversity, prevail against evil forces, and serve his country and king.

Onoda's instructions were simple and direct, so he followed. Unfortunately, his mission met with overwhelming opposition from the Allied powers, and he retreated into the region's jungles. Under his direct supervision, Hiroo

Onoda and the survivors remained oblivious to the war's outcome yet held their vow to their compatriots to continue the fight and contribute by any means necessary. Over three decades, the few who remained in the company of Onoda adopted the strategies of guerrilla warfare, carrying out secret missions that killed over 30 Philippine law enforcement officers and civilians, engaged in several shootouts, and an array of outdated war strategies in the name of the Japanese army. For years, leaflets were dropped from aircrafts into the jungle with the message, "The war ended on the 15th of August 1947. Come down from the mountains!" However, Hiro and the three remaining men inferred that this was false propaganda orchestrated by the Western troops and refused to yield.

Countless letters and pictures from the families of estranged soldiers were also airdropped into the jungle, but the comrades, bound by their oaths, did not yield. As the altercations with fishermen, farmers, and the occasional law enforcement officer prevailed, the band of soldiers dwindled as they got picked off one after the other. By the 19th of October 1972, Lieutenant Hiroo Onoda was, to his knowledge, the sole survivor, and was compelled to carry on fighting. He had been instructed to die fighting, but under no circumstance was he allowed to take his own life.

For years, Onoda remained in that jungle, surviving amidst animals, foraging for sustenance, and carrying out what he believed to be his sole purpose in life. He had no luxuries, companions, or connection to the outside world except for blind faith that the Imperial Army would rescue him if he continued to do his part. On the 20th of February 1974, a peculiar explorer named Norio Suzuki found the immortalized martyr and local legend Hiroo in the Philippines' wilderness, revealing to him the truth of the outside world. After much convincing and a visit from his former commanding officer to reassure him of the historical progression of the Second World War, Hiroo Onoda laid down his arms and ended his tour.

The story of a war hero who was left alone in the jungle, fighting a war that had ended long ago, had become the talk of the town. The most renowned media establishments, such as BBC and CNN, covered the heroic tale of the Japanese lieutenant who spent the majority of his life in hiding and dedicated himself to an oath that was long fulfilled. The story of his '10,000 nights' spread like wildfire across the globe. The entertainment industry even produced a biopic about him, and of course, Hiroo wrote a book about his time, which became a bestseller. He grew somewhat of a celebrity status in Japan, an icon, and a heroic tale memorialized in military propaganda. Hiro completed the most challenging task of his life and was now enjoying the fruits of his labor. His victory parade consisted of talk show interviews, public appearances, and documented statements in which Onoda declared that he felt no regret over the years spent in the jungle, living off insects and vegetation and deprived of any luxuries or riches. He had an unwavering sense of purpose, and his path to achieving his goal kept him hopeful and persistent through all the inhumane suffering he endured. Fame, money, power, and social admiration were not his priorities but rather the successful completion of his mission.

In 1980, less than five years after returning to the country he fought so relentlessly for, Hiroo Onoda packed his bags and moved 17,360 km away to Brazil, where he died in 2014. But how could someone who showed so much love and devotion to his motherland emancipate himself from the very people he went to war for? The answer was simple: he could not find meaning and purpose in his new life in Japan. He claimed that the values and philosophies of the country he was accustomed to had vanished, and the new world contradicted the core morals he believed in. In addition to all of this, his disconnect with the evolving culture of the world left him tone-deaf to the 20th century, rendering him a figure of the past to be admired but not welcomed into the future. Ironically, Onoda's mental well-being deteriorated in the bustling, interconnected world, a state that he claimed never came to fruition in the lonely jungle. He chalked this up to the mission that he upheld day in and day out - a northern star that enabled him to continue onward towards a noble cause that he believed in wholeheartedly. Unable to stomach the directionless world he had stepped into, the man who endured 30 years of exile was left desiring the island he had been left stranded on.

What was even more comical was that the gentleman who had rescued Onoda from the jungle, Norio Suzuki, was a university dropout who traveled the world due to his dissatisfaction with the facade of modern society, searching for "Lieutenant Onoda, a panda, and the Abominable Snowman, in that order." Suzuki wholeheartedly believed in his exploration, and he managed to discover the war hero who evaded the search efforts of three well-equipped nations. Norio went on to successfully find a panda, eventually dying in an avalanche in the Himalayas while looking for the Abominable Snowman.

The purpose of this tale isn't to mock Suzuki for dying in search of a fictional character or to praise the bravery of Onoda's pointless and adamant struggle in the jungle. It is to indicate the outlandish things that give people meaning. The Wright Brothers wanted to fly, which was delusional at the time, yet they devoted their lives to the cause. Michelangelo almost went blind obsessing over the Sistine Chapel and his other works of art. Religious followers still believe that they will be judged after death, sentencing them to eternal bliss or damnation, sometimes to the point of extremism. We all have a multitude of different things that give us meaning in our lives. Some ideas are ridiculed or misunderstood, yet they give us a sense of purpose driven by passion.

"I think as human beings, by nature as a species, we're all flawed. We have to constantly ask ourselves the uncomfortable questions. Is the world better from me having been in it? Rather than change the world to suit our needs better, how can we change ourselves to better suit the world we all live in, thoughtfully examining the roles we play? How to best be of use and be of service in a noble pursuit to make the world a better place? I believe perfection is unattainable, but that doesn't stop us from trying. We should constantly evolve, redefine, refine, predict, analyze, and adapt to whatever the world throws at us. Suppose one is passionate and committed to the noble pursuit of excellence within their chosen field, be that the arts, technology, science, humanitarianism, or conservationism; then I would say one has a moral obligation and an ethical duty to be of service and always to strive to be part of the solution and not the problem. After all, it's a world that our children would inherit, and that's worth being a part of. That speaks to me. Passion, Action, and Noble Intention create progress. Passion creates progress."
- *Tom Hardy*

Perspective Vs. Perception

I am an avid moviegoer, and I love the cinema experience. The controlled lighting, perfect volume levels, large viewing surface, comfortable reclining seats, blankets, and overpriced processed food all contribute to a wonderful experience. It's vastly different from watching a movie at home on your TV. Film purists argue that a movie's plot significance is lost when viewed outside of a movie auditorium. They believe that the director's vision, the musician's score, and the actor's nuances are best appreciated in the streamlined environment intended by the creators.

Currently, the entertainment industry is buzzing about the movie 'Dune: Part 2'. Before watching it myself, I read some of its overwhelmingly positive reviews, with many calling it a masterpiece of filmmaking. This excited me, so I went to watch it at the cinema with a friend. I loved the movie so much that I went back to watch it again a week later. My friend, however, fell asleep within 30 minutes of the runtime. She claimed the 'Barbie' movie with Ryan Gosling and Margot Robbie was more entertaining, which deeply offended me.

Furthermore, some video reviews criticized the story of 'Dune: Part 2' as being about a white savior and lacking representation. They listed various issues fueled by 'cancel culture,' which had risen in the early 21st century. I found it perplexing how a cautionary tale about political and religious manipulation could be so misconstrued as a white savior narrative. I was amused by the serious tone people took with a science fiction film based on a novel about interplanetary war. I even witnessed an interview with a decorated scientist debating the accuracy of the movement of a giant fictional worm that the characters ride as a mode of transportation. The stark contrast in interpreting the core ideas and principles of the story was like comparing night and day.

There is a point to the nerdy rant I just made you endure. To understand it, we must first define two key terms:

Perspective: *n.* *"Perspective is the individual's point of view that shapes their perception of the world and influences their opinions about themselves, others, and everything else around them."*

Perception: *n.* *"Perception is the interpretation and understanding of a situation, person, or object, which is the meaning assigned to any given stimulus."*

Which is more important in shaping our beliefs: perspective or perception? At first glance, it may seem that our perspective, our personal point of view, governs how we perceive the world around us. However, the truth is quite different. It is our perception of reality that shapes our perspective. Our perspectives are based on our perceptions, which are inextricably linked to our beliefs. Forming beliefs is a nuanced process, often shaped by repeated exposure or intense emotional encounters. Once these beliefs are formed, they become the lens through which we interpret our experiences and environment.

This repeated exposure to sensory interpretation forms our opinions, beliefs, values, morals, core drivers, and, most importantly, the physical actions and choices we make on a regular basis. Consuming information through social media, mainstream news, daily interactions with people, and the culture of our surrounding environments, all play a crucial role in molding our experiences and, as a result, our perspective on life.

When trying to change the way you see things, it's vital to first understand the beliefs and opinions that shape your perspective. Instead of immediately trying to change your point of view, it's more effective to work on the fundamental beliefs and opinions that inform it. People often hold strong attachments to their beliefs and viewpoints, so any efforts to encourage a shift in perspective should be approached with positivity, support, and a focus on personal values.

This chapter aims to challenge your perspective — not on your personal views or political opinions, but on how certain you are of yourself. I want to alter your perception by providing an understanding of the beauty of uncertainty.

Historically, the importance of experience as a catalyst for growth has been widely emphasized. Job experience builds careers, emotional understanding matures individuals, and social expertise fosters relationships. The list goes on. Over time, the diverse experiences we have endured over a considerable period enable our brain to create associations and patterns, helping us learn appropriate responses to stimuli. In fact, this learning process has been a crucial path for humanity and has significantly contributed to our evolution as the apex predator of the planet.

In the pre-agricultural and pre-industrial eras, animals that failed to recognize the danger posed by Homo sapiens faced extinction. Species that did not evolve a fear response to humans or adapt quickly enough were hunted and eventually eradicated. This phenomenon highlights our significant impact on ecosystems and the extinction of various species, including other apex predators when they failed to develop a fear of humans or were unable to coexist with them.

Today, with the emergence of technology and our growing disconnect from physical-experiential knowledge, we face a similar risk that the very animals we drove to extinction did. But now, the threat comes from a better-equipped version of ourselves. I don't advocate the extreme teachings of self-help gurus who demand waking up at 5 AM and working tirelessly until 11 PM. Nor do I suggest that you should voluntarily expose yourself to all of life's trauma and hardship, hoping to interpret your psychological scars as mental fortitude against the harsh world.

A healthier perspective is to remain open to the idea that you might be wrong about everything. The effect of new information in enacting change and refining your ability to respond to circumstances - both favorable and detrimental - depends on your ability to acknowledge your own shortcomings and misunderstandings. This approach creates a necessary divide between oneself and complete certainty.

"The cleverest of all, in my opinion,
is the man who calls himself a fool
at least once a month."
- Fyodor Dostoevsky.

Take the English language, for example. My sentence structure may seem proper to you and me. I may not be perfect, but I like to think I use grammar and comprehension proficiently. For years, I have been taught to speak, write, and understand the language in a particular way. However, linguists argue that alternate dialects of English are equally correct, and the place and context dictate which dialect is appropriate.

For example, consider this accepted conversation in Singapore between two colleagues discussing their lunch order:

Person 1: "*Eh*, what you want to makan for lunch *uh*?"

("What would you like to have for lunch?")

Person 2: "Cin cai *lor*, Cai Peng? Nasi Padang? Or the ah neh stall?"

("I am open to any food options. How about Chinese Economic Rice, which is a Malay version of mixed rice that originated from Indonesia? Or should we go to the Indian stall?")

Person 1: "I feel like dabao-ing *leh*, I have a tele-conference with the Ang-moh client at 2 PM. Sian *sia*."

("I will most likely have a takeaway, as I have a tele-conference with a client at 2 PM. I'm dreading it.")

Person 2: "Walao, if not we tumpang Jess to buy *lor*. They're at the kopitiam now."

("Oh! How about we ask Jess if they can help us get takeaway? They're at the coffee shop now!")

Person 1: "Can *hor*, liddat I want Satay Beehoon, with teh-c kosong peng!"

("Oh, that's fine! I would like to order Satay Beehoon, which is rice vermicelli topped with a chili-based peanut sauce. Additionally, please get me an iced tea made with evaporated milk and without sugar.")

We see here that the Singlish dialect may be incomprehensible to an Englishman trained under the conditions of the Queen's English. But which one is right? Sure, the Western dialect of the language is more commonly spoken; it may be associated with higher socioeconomic classes and perceived as a sign of literacy. However, in varying contexts, the Singaporean dialect may be more appropriate.

The passage above might sound like slang used in the region, and many places worldwide have a unique array of informal jargon in their vocabulary. When used over an extended time period by an increasing number of people, that version of the language becomes the norm through majority adoption. The Queen's English itself is an adaptation of Latin. We don't speak like Shakespeare in 2024, and the Victorian era didn't use English like their ancestors did. Words such as bizarre, brunette, cafe, ballet, and chauffeur were all derived from French. Words like aberration, democratic, enthusiasm, imaginary, and juvenile were adopted from Latin.

The very language you speak, or at least the way you communicate, is different in different parts of the world. So, you may be correct momentarily and be wrong in the future. If something as fundamental as your primary means of communication constantly evolves, then your understanding of the world must also develop. It is crucial to grow alongside these changes.

Certainly, nobody enjoys being told that they are always wrong. However, within the vast tapestry of Stoic philosophy, the virtue of being wrong is presented as an asset. It embodies humility, resilience, integrity, and an unwavering pursuit of wisdom. At its core lies a profound understanding of our human fallibility; it acknowledges that we are imperfect beings navigating the complexities of existence.

Epictetus argues that we must recognize the dichotomy of control, which involves distinguishing between what is within our control and what is not. In other words, it is about acknowledging the limits of our influence in any given situation and taking firm control of our thoughts and actions, even in the face of inevitable mistakes. Individuals who exhibit a high degree of certainty in themselves, their beliefs, and their actions are often prone to making mistakes due to their uninformed optimism. These are usually people who seek self-esteem, like politicians, celebrities, and business executives who get used to being praised and become overconfident in their abilities.

The way we see and interpret the world is complex and deeply intertwined with personality traits such as Narcissism, Machiavellianism, and subclinical Psychopathy. Those who display these traits tend to prioritize their own needs and desires over the well-being of others, leading to a distorted view of the world. Although individuals with these traits may excel in leadership roles due to their confidence and charisma, their manipulative tendencies can harm team morale and cohesion. In personal relationships, their lack of empathy and concern for others' well-being can lead to dysfunctional dynamics characterized by power struggles and emotional manipulation.

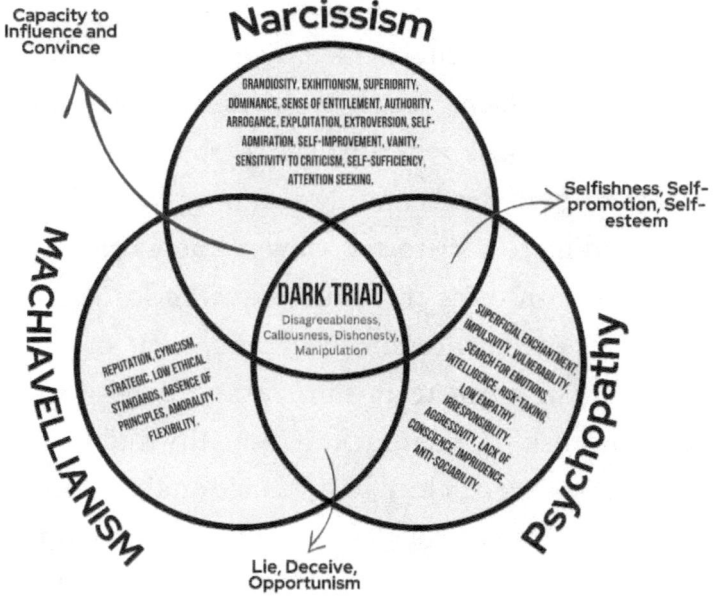

Individuals who possess dark triad traits often find it challenging to regulate their emotions effectively, leading to heightened levels of anger, impulsivity, and hostility. Despite appearing confident on the outside, they have deep-seated insecurities and vulnerabilities that drive their constant pursuit of external validation and control. This need for admiration and control stems from their fear of rejection and a distorted view of their own self-worth, creating a cycle of emotional turmoil and interpersonal dysfunction.

Individuals with dark triad traits can exhibit resistance to change due to their strong attachment to their beliefs and perceptions. It is essential to recognize how repeated exposure and intense emotional encounters can shape one's beliefs and perspectives, as well as the influence of external factors such as cultural norms, news consumption, and social media. Social media platforms have become a breeding ground for the proliferation and reinforcement of dark triad personality traits. Firstly, these platforms prioritize self-promotion and validation through metrics such as likes, comments, and shares, creating an environment conducive to narcissistic tendencies. Users are incentivized to curate and present idealized versions of themselves, often portraying an exaggerated sense of accomplishment, attractiveness, and triumph to gain admiration and approval from their online peers. Constant comparison with the carefully curated highlight reels of others can exacerbate feelings of inadequacy and fuel the relentless pursuit of external validation, further reinforcing narcissistic behaviors.

Secondly, social media platforms provide a facilitative environment for Machiavellianism by offering anonymity and detachment that foster deceptive and manipulative behaviors. Individuals with Machiavellian tendencies may exploit the anonymity of social media to engage in strategic manipulation, such as spreading misinformation, orchestrating smear campaigns, or manipulating online interactions to advance their agendas. The vast reach and instant circulation of information on social media enable Machiavellian individuals to manipulate narratives and shape public opinion to suit their objectives, often at the expense of truth and integrity.

Overall, social media's pervasive influence and structural features contribute to the amplification and reinforcement of dark triad personality traits. This perpetuates a culture of superficiality, self-centeredness, and manipulation, undermining genuine self-worth, emotional stability, and ethical standards in online interactions.

> *"A man who lies to himself and believes his own*
> *lies becomes unable to recognize truth,*
> *either in himself or in anyone else,*
> *and he ends up losing respect for himself*
> *and for others. When he has no respect for any-*
> *one, he can no longer love, and,*
> *in order to divert himself, having no love in him,*
> *he yields to his impulses, indulges*
> *in the lowest forms of pleasure,*
> *and behaves in the end like an animal.*
> *And it all comes from lying - lying to*
> *others and to yourself."*
> *- Fyodor Dostoevsky.*

Ultimately, the journey toward personal growth and emotional maturity necessitates a willingness to confront and challenge one's existing beliefs and perceptions. True wisdom comes from your ability to be delighted when proven wrong and to perceive the setback as a positive moment of reflective learning, as opposed to a negative circumstance that requires self-resentment/doubt.

Throughout our lives, we tend to experience more than our fair share of stress, which multiplies daily with the increase in global connectivity. Taking a positive approach to stress management means embracing it as a natural part of life and learning to navigate it healthily.

"Uncertainty is the root of all progress
and all growth."
- Mark Manson.

Uncertainty is not a foe to be defeated but a guiding light illuminating the path to growth and self-discovery. Even the greatest movie villains, those archetypes of unwavering certainty who cling rigidly to their beliefs and agendas, fall because they refuse to entertain doubt and embrace the possibility of alternative truths. In contrast, uncertainty serves as fertile soil from which seeds of personal evolution and enlightenment sprout. It propels us out of our comfort zones, forcing us to confront our limitations and challenge our assumptions.

In the realm of uncertainty, we are liberated from the shackles of dogma and empowered to explore the boundless potential of our own existence. Pursuing certainty is an unsafe journey that often leads to the dark abyss of Narcissism, Machiavellianism, and Psychopathy—the unholy trinity of the human psyche. Embracing uncertainty cultivates humility, empathy, and resilience in the fertile soil of doubt.

The Backwards Law

As a member of Generation Z, born between 1990 and 2010, my generation is entering the workforce or moving beyond stages of dependency in life—at the time of writing. However, I have noticed a lot of criticism suggesting that our generation needs to be more active, prepared, and realistic in our perception of everyday life. But every generation complains about the next one. Perhaps the world we inherit from our predecessors is more complex, and each generation needs to find new and intuitive ways to address societal complications and demands.

I have also observed that many of us in Gen Z share a sense of learned helplessness. We may have grown up watching the world fail and become accustomed to sensationalized cases of constant disappointment, victim narratives, and biased information systems designed to complicate our lives. Information providers curate negative emotions in us, which grab and retain our attention. In addition, a social system that fosters anti-social tendencies and self-centeredness has diluted our understanding of meaning and purpose.

We now see the world as an economic game, where nuclear families and marriages are viewed as financial burdens. Social and dating lives have become paid-to-play privileges, hierarchically based on monetary and social capital. Adolescents can now view and compare their lives to millions of people every day, and employers can sift through the globe for potential candidates. The technological ease of discovery has over-complicated relationships with peers and partners. As a result, we are bombarded with self-help gurus and other individuals urging us to work harder and endure the early years of our lives to become high-value individuals. Independence, career planning, and self-sustainability are sensationalized as paths to a happier life in the distant future, contingent on forgoing the present and sentencing ourselves to isolated suffering.

The particular phenomenon I am referring to is called the arrival fallacy.

According to Tal Ben Shahar, the arrival fallacy is the false assumption that once you reach a goal, you will experience enduring happiness. The tendency to fetishize suffering and sacrifice is not a new world concept. Our parents and grandparents often spin tales about how hard they had to work and sacrifice to provide the life we 'take for granted.' We have all been compared to or compared ourselves to other successful and hardworking individuals, attempting to recreate their victory by emulating their work ethic or mindset. The world loves to romanticize the suffering and hardship of others to inspire the masses, and we tend to get motivated as planned. Unfortunately, this sets a false precedent; to achieve anything and be happy, we must suffer, work tirelessly, sacrifice comforts, and outwork the world.

I saw a tweet by Chris Williamson the other day, and it went something like this:

> "I've been thinking about people who succeed at things they don't enjoy. We sacrifice what we want (happiness) for the thing that is supposed to get it (success). If we make ourselves miserable in pursuing success because we believe that success will make us happy, why not just shortcut everything and do something we enjoy? Is your happiness aimed at fulfilling you? Or impressing everyone else?
>
> 'This is an extra special type of tragedy that unfolds while everyone cheers. Strangling your passions in exchange for an elite life is like being on the Titanic after the iceberg, drowning up to your chin, with everybody telling you you're so lucky to be on the greatest steamship of all time. And the Titanic is indeed so huge and wonderful that you can't help but agree, but you're also feeling a bit cold and wet, and you're not sure why.' - Adam Mastroianni.
>
> What is the point of success if the road to get there is paved with nails? The journey is the destination. Don't strangle your passions in return for an elite life."

The 'Backward Law' was coined by philosopher Alan Watts, who proposed that the more we pursue something, the more we achieve the opposite of what we truly want - leading to disappointment. In simpler terms, the harder we try, the less likely we are to succeed. On the other hand, when we stop trying so hard, we may finally get what we want. This may sound ironic, but it is true. When we try to control our habits and impulses, we often become frustrated, which can worsen the problem. Instead, accepting our emotions, failures, faults, and inadequacies can help us be more considerate of ourselves and gain more control over our impulses.

A man named David Goggins attempted to run an ultra marathon after suffering fractures in both his legs, and his kidneys failed three-fourths of the way through the race. However, Goggins preaches visualization and self-talk as the motivational factor that got him through the remaining 30 miles of the race. Let's face reality for a second: you and I are not ex-navy seals trained to endure torturous amounts of pain and persevere through; David Goggins is a 240-pound veteran. And yes, Goggins did finish the marathon and go on multiple podcasts to tell the story. Yes, it's very inspiring, but he was also miserable and suffered through the whole race.

Don't try to run an ultramarathon with the time you have, breaking bones, voluntarily destroying the vital factors of your life in hopes that the finish line will result in everything you ever wanted.

Remember the Backward Law: happiness is not found in its pursuit; instead, accepting dissatisfaction can lead to greater happiness. Seeking absolute security only fuels insecurity, while embracing uncertainty fosters a sense of safety. Trying to compel love and acceptance from others diminishes both our self-love and their regard for us. Respect is earned through giving it, not demanding it. Trust is reciprocated when freely given rather than forced. Striving for confidence often leads to heightened insecurity; accepting our flaws promotes self-assurance. Constantly seeking self-improvement breeds feelings of inadequacy; self-acceptance fosters growth and evolution.

The human condition is characterized by an insatiable will to live, which drives us to constantly seek more but ultimately leaves us feeling unfulfilled. This perpetual pursuit can only be transcended by relinquishing desire altogether. True contentment lies in accepting imperfection and embracing the present moment without constantly striving for more. By letting go of the constant pursuit of external goals and desires, we can find peace and fulfillment in what already exists.

Letting go of an identity or perception of yourself is hard, but evolving and finding meaning in your existence is necessary. This shift in perspective, from seeking to not wanting, allows us to break free from the hedonic cycle of dissatisfaction and experience genuine happiness. Ultimately, by embracing the backward law and cultivating a state of 'not wanting,' we can uncover a more profound sense of joy and fulfillment in the present moment.

Misalignment Burnout

The World Health Organization defines 'burnout' as:

"A syndrome conceptualized as resulting from chronic workplace stress that has not been successfully managed. Three dimensions characterize it:

- *Feelings of exhaustion or energy depletion.*
- *An increased sense of mental distance from one's job, along with feelings of negativity or cynicism related to that job.*
- *Reduced professional efficacy."*

If you persist in pursuing a particular career or lifestyle, you may experience one of three types of burnout. The first type is overexertion burnout, which results from the mental and physical strain caused by stress and overworking. The second type is depletion burnout, which occurs when you maintain a demanding routine for prolonged periods without taking breaks or time to recharge. Finally, misalignment burnout happens when you engage in activities or work in environments that clash with your core values and beliefs, creating a disconnect between your authentic self and professional identity.

According to a survey conducted in 2023, a significant number of Americans, especially those belonging to the Gen Z (79%) and millennial (65%) age groups, are currently experiencing burnout. This is often due to prioritizing external rewards, such as financial gain and societal validation, over internal motivations and personal fulfillment. While these actions may seem reasonable for short-term success, they can jeopardize long-term goals and individual satisfaction, leading to emotional exhaustion and burnout. Research has demonstrated the importance of aligning personal values with organizational culture. Individuals who strongly connect with their roles and work environments are less vulnerable to burnout. Misalignment burnout not only affects mental and physical health but also reduces work performance, impacting productivity, creativity, and interpersonal relationships, thus compromising overall well-being.

We tell ourselves a false narrative that the exceptionally disciplined and hardworking are the successful and happy ones. However, there is little to be gained by forcing yourself to do something you don't enjoy. Most ordinary people can't and won't ever cultivate the mental fortitude to make extreme changes. A radical change or objective reflection usually happens at the tail end of a crisis or your worst moments, forcing you to reflect. You shouldn't shield yourself from a natural series of occurrences that lead to objective reflection, but neither should you seek out pain and suffering in hopes of being enlightened and forced into a purpose-filled life.

We do what we want to do, and we pursue things that mean something to us. For example, a fisherman who loves to sail will enjoy his life far more than an investment banker who despises his working conditions. Irrespective of money, power, fame, social status, and all that comes with an elite lifestyle, it is a journey that was paved with nails, where you didn't take moments to just exist in bliss. Like Suzuki dedicating his life to finding the endangered panda, a lost soldier, or even the irrational hunt for the abominable snowman, we must feel optimistic about the things we want to do. To truly experience and achieve the utopian version of your perfect life, you need to acknowledge and identify what is important to you.

The life you lead will be the life you focus on; a content and satisfied human being will concentrate on the factors that make them happy rather than the multitude of things that could cause dissatisfaction. Suppose you are unhappy and unsatisfied in life. In that case, no matter how great it may be, you will continue to focus on the negatives, unable to acknowledge or show gratitude towards the outstanding things. Our brains generalize and associate daily with whatever we focus on. There will always be things you want, and obsessing over them constantly, and suffering to achieve these wants, will result in a lack of enjoyment in the present, fueling a pathological need to be successful due to a crippling feeling of inadequacy.

When people talk about addiction, it usually refers to a habit that facilitates long-term harm, such as smoking, intoxication, drugs, or porn. However, it is rarely considered an addiction when it comes to habits that lead to productive or positive outcomes. An Olympic marathon runner is addicted to the training and experience of physical exertion, a skydiving expert is addicted to adrenaline, and a workaholic is addicted to relentless effort. No one criticizes the person who works day and night if they are somewhat of a success: athletes, entrepreneurs, or experts in their field. Their efforts are glorified and immortalized as tales of inspiration. These people aren't motivated by their love for hard work but are rather motivated by a feeling of inadequacy fueled by a pathological need to become someone of value, hoping for a dystopian future where they will feel a certain way and people around them will treat them a certain way. Simply put, they wanted to be loved but received adulation in return. Adulation is conditional in nature; we solicit admiration and praise in exchange for the incredible things we work tirelessly to make a reality.

The Pythagorean cup is a drinking vessel with a clever mechanism designed to punish those who pour too much liquid into it. If the liquid level rises above a certain point, the siphoning effect is triggered, causing the cup's contents to drain out. The person attempting to drink from the cup is surprised and frustrated by the sudden draining of the liquid. The Pythagorean cup is a meaningful symbol of moderation and self-restraint that carries an essential message. Its purpose is to remind individuals to be mindful of their actions and avoid excessive indulgence. If someone fills the cup beyond its capacity, the liquid will spill out, resulting in wastage. Similarly, if someone indulges excessively in anything, they might face negative consequences. Therefore, the cup serves as a potent reminder to practice moderation.

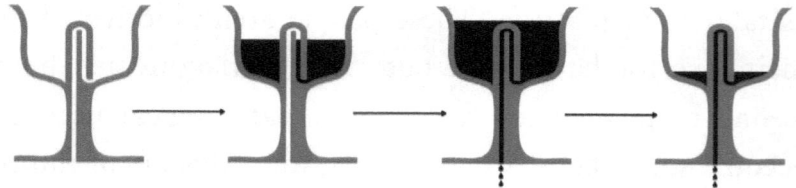

In the constant pursuit of adulation, the same acts of greatness are never sufficient to retain the misunderstood love and admiration of others. As a result, we must continually find bigger and better ways to generate the desired reaction from external sources. The more we fill our cups, the more they drain, but without the liquid in the vessel, we will die of thirst.

This is typical in hyper-successful individuals who don't exactly fit in, driving them to seek a sense of belonging through adoration from others. They become trapped and addicted to a perpetual cycle of outdoing themselves in an attempt to awe the masses and be loved. The desire to be anything - anyone - should come from internal necessities rather than external validation. Self-esteem must be a path toward self-actualization rather than backward integration to accumulate excessive social validation, status, or money.

The realization that external validation has never yielded a perpetual state of happiness, and the only way forward is to shed one's desire to acquire an abundance of things that misalign with one's natural desires, is the path forward.

Immortality Projects

Sonnet 73 of 154:

"*That time of year thou mayst in me behold*

When yellow leaves, or none, or few, do hang

Upon those boughs which shake against the cold,

Bare ruin'd choirs, where late the sweet birds sang.

In me, thou seest the twilight of such day

As after sunset fadeth in the west,

Which by and by black night doth take away,

Death's second self, that seals up all in rest.

In me, thou seest the glowing of such fire

That on the ashes of his youth doth lie,

As the death-bed whereon it must expire,

Consumed with that which it was nourished by.

This thou perceivest, which makes thy
love more strong,

To love that well which thou must leave ere long."

- *William Shakespeare.*

There comes a time when you feel it deep in your bones, in the very marrow of your existence: that moment when you realize you're no longer as young as you once were. It's not just the creaks in your joints or the lines etched into your skin; it's something deeper and more profound. In his sonnet, Shakespeare wrote about that time of year when leaves start to wither and fall, when nature begins its slow descent into winter's cold embrace. It's a metaphor for aging and facing the inevitable decay of our own bodies. He paints a picture of once vibrant choirs, now bare and ruined, and once vibrant places, now silent and empty. Much like all of us, as we grow older, the world around us starts to fade away.

It's not only about the body's deterioration; it's also about the relentless passage of time — time that never stops and leads toward the final moments of life. Shakespeare discusses death not as a distant and surreal event but rather as an imminent and inescapable companion, always present and close, like the night that inevitably follows day. Despite the talk of decay and death, there is a beautiful glimmer of hope. He speaks of a love that becomes stronger when we realize it is temporary. It's as if he's saying that love endures even when we have limited time, like a flame flickering against the darkness of death. Imagine a world where belief in immortality has faded, where life after death is merely a myth. A bleak landscape where the fear of death overshadows every part of our lives.

Ernest Becker's "The Denial of Death" is a work that explores the human psyche and the effects of our knowledge of our own mortality. Becker vividly portrays the burden of consciousness, showing how our realization of our inevitable death affects our lives in many ways. It influences our perceptions, motivations, and relationships, casting a long shadow over our existence. Becker's thesis highlights that human consciousness separates us from other beings on Earth. Unlike animals, who live in the present moment without understanding their own mortality, humans have a distinctive awareness of their inevitable death. This awareness, instead of being empowering, can be burdensome, serving as a constant reminder of our limited existence.

The curse of consciousness makes us acutely aware of the fragility of life and the ephemeral nature of our existence. It awakens within us a primal fear, a deep-seated dread of our own mortality. This fear manifests in various forms - the fear of aging, illness, and loss. It lurks in the shadows of our subconscious, coloring our thoughts, influencing our actions, and shaping our perception of the world.

One of the most profound consequences of this awareness is the stark dichotomy between our physical and conceptual selves. On one hand, we inhabit physical bodies bound by the laws of nature, subject to decay, disease, and eventual death. On the other hand, we possess a conceptual self, an abstract entity that transcends the limits of our physical existence. This conceptual self grapples with the notion of immortality, yearning for transcendence beyond the confines of our mortal loop.

Humans often struggle with the fact that they are mortal beings. To counter this existential dilemma, they engage in what is known as "immortality projects." These projects involve attempting to transcend death in some way, whether through religion, building a legacy, seeking fame and fortune, plastering your family name on a building, having children, and so on. Such projects function as psychological defense mechanisms, offering hope and meaning in the face of death.

With the rise of digital technology, we have created elaborate online personas that exist in cyberspace. The modern immortality project. These digital versions of ourselves are carefully curated and often seek validation and connection through likes, follows, and other forms of virtual approval. However, beneath this curated facade lies a disconnect between our digital selves and our true essence. Despite the illusion of immortality that the digital realm offers, we find ourselves increasingly disconnected from our authentic selves as we strive to maintain these carefully crafted personas. This often leads to a never-ending cycle of comparison and validation-seeking, further distancing us from who we truly are.

The discrepancy between our online selves and our true selves can lead to burnout and mental health issues.

We often strive for perfection and pretend to be happy and prosperous, but in reality, we are overwhelmed by our own expectations and the pressure to conform to society's standards. Our constant need for validation and approval can leave us drained and depleted. This cycle of striving and struggling can trap us in our immortality projects, but we must acknowledge the fleeting nature of life and find meaning in it. By pursuing immortality, we risk losing sight of life's beauty. We must embrace our mortality to appreciate the precious moments we have left. We should live each moment to its fullest, knowing that our time on this Earth is finite, but our impact on the world can endure long after we're gone.

*"If you were to destroy in mankind
the belief in immortality, not only love
but every living force maintaining the life
of the world would at once be dried up."*
- Fyodor Dostoevsky

PART THREE

REVELATION

CHAPTER 6

MIRRORED SOUL

In the previous chapters, the writing emphasized the individual's values, behavior, and the concept of metacognition on a micro-scale. It highlighted the significance of having values and aligning your behavior with them while being mindful of your needs, wants, and immediate surroundings. The remaining few chapters transcend a singular point of view, adopting a macro perspective in order to observe and understand social dynamics, culture, and the overall effect of the world on you and your ability to truly adopt a metacognitive mindset.

Mimetic Theory

In my quest to understand general behavior, I often found myself navigating a maze of conflicting theories in philosophy or psychological frameworks. These theories, supported by empirical studies and data-driven conclusions, often offer divergent resolutions to the same problems. There may never be a 'one size fits all' solution to the complex nature of our consciousness. But there are always patterns - patterns of behavior and general strategies that help explain the root causes of why we think the way we think. What makes us tick as a species?

One explanation that attempts to illuminate the path to profound or potentially transformative self-awareness is the Mimetic Theory by René Girard.

1. Mimetic Desire:

Mimetic theory aims to explain how human desire works and how it shapes our identity. According to this theory, desire is not something innate but rather something we learn through observation and imitation of others. We observe and mimic the desires of our parents, peers, and role models, which helps us internalize societal norms and values. This mimetic process not only influences our preferences but also creates a sense of rivalry as we compete for the same objects of desire. Mimetic theory is based on the understanding that desire is a fundamental force that drives human behavior and forms the basis of human relationships and societal structures.

> *"Man is the creature who does not know what to desire, and he turns to others in order to make up his mind. We desire what others desire because we imitate their desires."*
> *- René Girard.*

René Girard, a young man in his early twenties, was wrapping up college when he fell in love with a woman in Paris. Their relationship gained momentum, and before he knew it, his partner was ready for marriage. However, René was unprepared for that kind of commitment and ended the relationship. Like many teenagers who break up with their high school girlfriends, without the foresight that they will both eventually have to see other people, young Girard was consumed by a mix of emotions. He broke off the relationship because he had no desire to marry her, but suddenly, he wanted her back more than ever. The answer was not because she was a better fit for him than before, or because her character or personality had changed, and not even because she was physically more attractive. The answer was simple: it was seeing other men with his ex-girlfriend who no longer wanted him. This real-life scenario is a perfect example of Mimetic Desire in action, where the desire for a person is influenced by the desire of others.

This obviously triggered feelings of envy, insecurity, or even a heightened desire to win her back or prove himself superior to the other suitors. Mimetic desire in this context involves desiring qualities or characteristics assimilated by the ex-girlfriend and desiring the attention, validation, or perceived status associated with being in a relationship with her. For example, suppose you observe other men who appear to be successful, attractive, or compatible with your ex-girlfriend. In that case, you might feel compelled to emulate their qualities or achievements in an attempt to regain her interest or outshine the competition. This could lead to rivalry or a longing to prove oneself worthy of her affection.

Furthermore, he realized that she had become the object of desire in his eyes, and her new boyfriend had become the 'model' to mirror and simultaneously a rival. A 'model' refers to a person or object that serves as a source of desire or imitation for an individual. By denying herself to Girard, the interest of third parties in her resulted in the modeling of what René should desire. This is exacerbated to the point where people develop 'a type' - a colloquial term for an individual who exhibits characteristics and traits that are perceived to be attractive to a particular person. This understanding of the 'model' concept in Mimetic Desire can help us comprehend the complex dynamics of human desire and its social implications.

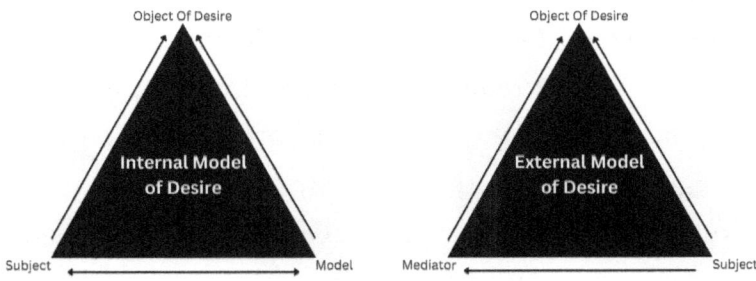

This phenomenon transcends the context of a relationship. Take the apparel industry, for example; people imitate what they perceive as desirable or fashionable, leading to the spread of particular styles or brands within society. We often desire products or services because others want them rather than for their inherent utility or quality. Celebrity culture is heavily influenced by mimetic desire through the mimicry of lifestyles, behaviors, or appearances of superstars. People admire these celebrities and are driven by a desire to attain similar status or recognition. This can lead to the emulation of celebrity style, speech patterns, or even life choices.

Political polarization is also an effect of Girard's theory, as individuals align themselves with certain ideologies or political figures based on imitation rather than critical analysis. The masses tend to adopt the views or behaviors of others within their social groups or communities, leading to the reinforcement of ideological divides. Mimetic desire is also evident in religious rituals and beliefs; followers may imitate the practices of others within their religious community, driven by a passion for spiritual fulfillment or social cohesion. This can lead to replicating and perpetuating religious traditions and customs over time.

2. Mimetic Rivalry:

Traditional economic theory is based on the idea that individuals seek to maximize their own utility and well-being, known as self-interest. The metaphor of the invisible hand, coined by Adam Smith, suggests that individuals unintentionally contribute to society's greater good by pursuing self-interest. Rationality is also a crucial element of this framework, where people are believed to make decisions through careful deliberation to maximize utility. However, in reality, human behavior often deviates from these idealized notions. Mimetic rivalry exposes the hidden forces at play as individuals become entangled in a web of desires shaped by the actions and aspirations of their peers. Instead of making rational decisions, people get trapped in a cycle of wanting to keep up with others.

Imagine a stock trader named John who is faced with a challenging task of navigating the unpredictable waters of financial markets. Initially, John approaches his investment decisions with a rational mindset, analyzing market trends and economic indicators conscientiously. However, as he observes the successes and failures of his colleagues, he finds himself increasingly influenced by their actions and desires. John becomes a victim of mimetic rivalry, which compels him to abandon his rational decision-making process and instead mirror the behaviors of his rivals.

As John gives in to his desire to imitate others, the previously stable dynamics of the market experience a subtle but noteworthy shift. Rationality is replaced by irrational exuberance or panic as traders engage in herd behavior, driven by the fear of missing out or the desire to outdo their competitors. The invisible hand, which was once believed to be all-powerful in guiding market equilibrium, now seems powerless in the face of the chaotic forces of mimetic rivalry.

Rivalry usually leads to conflict and scarcity. This is because mimetic desire is often fueled by factors such as exclusivity and rivalrous consumption, like fighting for the last slice of pizza. The solution to the mimetic rivalry is frequently 'scapegoating.'

3. Scapegoating:

Excessive desire to imitate others within a group can create tension, leading to the selection of a scapegoat. This scapegoat can be an individual or group unfairly blamed for the community's problems. The scapegoat is then expelled or even subjected to violence. This violence relieves the tension, bringing the community together against a common enemy and restoring social order.

For instance, the Sri Lankan Civil War, a brutal conflict that lasted for thirty years, can be understood through the concept of scapegoating. During British colonial rule in Sri Lanka, which spanned over a century, a divide-and-rule system was established. The British exploited existing ethnic and religious tensions between the Sinhalese majority and the Tamil minority, leading to unequal distribution of wealth, ethno-religious division, and a power-sharing mechanism based on rivalry.

In the aftermath of colonial rule, both Sinhalese and Tamil groups may have subconsciously replicated the dominance model that was observed during British rule, fueling a desire for power over the other, rather than addressing the root causes of the conflict. Scapegoating became increasingly common, with both sides resorting to propaganda to demonize the other group and depict them as a threat to national security and cultural identity. This created an atmosphere of fear and hatred, which led to outbreaks of violence against civilians and political leaders. Each violent act by one group was seen as a justification for further violence by the other, perpetuating a cycle of retribution with no end in sight. As the conflict escalated, individuals on both sides became more entrenched in their group identities, losing sight of the original causes of the conflict. The key to resolving the dispute was recognizing that the other group was not the true enemy but rather a fellow victim of a larger historical process.

Scapegoating is a powerful tool that creates a convincing illusion by hiding the true source of tension and guilt within a group. It achieves this by making everyone believe that the chosen victim is responsible for the problems. People who are involved in scapegoating genuinely believe that the victim caused the trouble, and they see the removal of the scapegoat as the reason for the calmness that follows. However, they fail to recognize the underlying act of violence – the scapegoating itself.

Girard's use of mimetic theory highlights an interesting case of rivalry and scapegoating in the history of the world—the story of Jesus Christ. Although I am not a religious person, religious scripture often captures social behavior quite elegantly in their efforts to pass on their teachings. In the story of Jesus, the religious authorities of the time held power and prestige based on their interpretation of religious law. When Jesus emerged, preaching a message of love, forgiveness, and a different relationship with God, he challenged their established order. People began to follow Jesus, mimicking his message and teachings, which created a mimetic rivalry. The religious leaders saw their power and influence threatened by Jesus' growing popularity. According to Girard, when mimetic rivalry intensifies, communities can become gripped by contagious violence. To restore social order, a scapegoat is chosen, and in this case, the religious leaders, fearing a loss of control, orchestrated Jesus' arrest and crucifixion. By scapegoating Jesus, they aimed to quell the growing movement he inspired and restore their own authority.

The Christian narrative is not just a simple story of scapegoating. Jesus' message of love and forgiveness provides an alternative to the cycle of violence. By accepting his fate willingly, Jesus exposed the injustice of the scapegoating mechanism and presented a way toward reconciliation and forgiveness.

Politicians often scapegoat entire groups of minorities or immigrants, blaming them for social or economic problems in an attempt to villainize their political rivals, painting them as unfit or even dangerous. This deflects attention away from potentially complex issues and rallies their base around a perceived common threat. In sports, fans or even the owners of their respective losing teams sometimes scapegoat a single player, the manager, or the referee to avoid acknowledging deeper problems within the organization.

4. The Perpetual Cycle:

Scapegoating may seem like a quick solution to social unrest, but it actually creates a vicious cycle. It perpetuates the very problems it seeks to solve and fuels the tensions that led to scapegoating in the first place. After the victim is ostracized or eliminated, the remaining group leads the formation of social structures that aim to prevent similar violence. These structures can be laws, taboos, and rituals, and they are often unconsciously a reenactment of the scapegoating itself. While these measures offer a sense of order, they fail to address the underlying issue: mimetic rivalry. In fact, these structures can worsen the problem by constantly reinforcing the 'us vs. them' mentality and reminding everyone of the scapegoated 'other' who caused the trouble.

The danger lies in the cyclical nature of this process. The person or group blamed for a problem becomes a symbol, a cautionary tale with no real learning. The underlying tensions remain unresolved, waiting for a new scapegoat when the next crisis hits. This pattern affects nations, communities, organizations, and even families. Each cycle strengthens the social structures built on this flawed foundation, creating a fragile stability that constantly teeters on the brink of renewed violence. We must confront the underlying issues driving the conflict to break free from this cycle. We need to foster empathy and understanding and address the true causes of tension rather than just finding convenient targets to blame.

We stand at the edge, looking down at the vast landscape of who we are. The map we held, with neatly labeled desires and unwavering beliefs, suddenly seems less authoritative.

Mimetic theory has revealed a shocking truth: our compass wasn't pointing north; it mimicked the explorer next door! Were the things we craved and the paths we deemed noble truly our own, or were they mere reflections of what others desired?

Is there anything authentic left? This isn't a dead end but a thrilling fork in the road. We can shed the borrowed desires and mimicked convictions like a heavy cloak. It's a chance to forge our own map, etched with the unique yearnings of our soul. It's a messy, exhilarating process, like hacking through a jungle to find a hidden oasis. Here, beneath the untamed canopy of our true selves, purpose whispers through the wind. Fulfillment isn't found in replicating another's happiness but in unearthing the wellspring of joy within. We savor experiences not because they're trendy but because they resonate with the music of our being. This authenticity, this freedom from mimetic shadows, is the key that unlocks the true treasures of life.

Cancel Culture

The six degrees of separation theory, also known as the "six handshake rule," suggests that any two individuals can be connected to each other through a "friend of a friend" network within an average of six steps.

In the 20th century, American psychologist Stanley Milgram created a real-world model called the "Small World Theory." Milgram conducted an experiment where he asked random strangers to transfer a package to someone they knew, who would then pass it on until it finally reached a stranger in Boston, who was known only by name and occupation. It was expected that the chain would involve hundreds of intermediaries before the package arrived at the intended recipient in Boston. However, in multiple rounds of testing, the average number of intermediaries turned out to be only five to seven people. It's worth noting that this experiment involved a physical package that was shared one at a time in 1967.

It is now 2024, and communication channels have come a long way from wired telephones and physical parcels delivered by mailing systems. Transmission infrastructure, governed by the principles of separation theory, is now used to map complex databases such as power grids, disease transmission routes, and search engine optimization. The world is more interconnected than ever before. A study by Zhimin Zhang and colleagues on the impact of the internet and social media posed the question of whether the "six degrees" rule still applies. Interestingly, they found that online connections can actually be even shorter, with an average of four to three and a half degrees of separation on social media. This means that it typically takes fewer "friend of a friend" intermediaries to connect with someone online compared to the real world. Social media allows us to expand our circles far beyond our immediate surroundings, making it easier to find those crucial connections.

This bottleneck of separation between oneself and the rest of the world, with all its information and unlimited desires, is a recipe for disaster when viewed through the perspective of Mimetic Theory. While fostering a sense of closeness, hyper-connectivity has paradoxically ushered in an era of information overload, rivalry, and even mental health concerns. Social media platforms function within the "attention economy," where our limited engagement is the most valuable commodity. Algorithms, fueled by our clicks and likes, curate a never-ending stream of content designed to trigger dopamine release, the brain's reward chemical. This creates a feedback loop: we crave the positive reinforcement of likes and comments, leading us to seek out more content, perpetuating the cycle.

In today's world, where everyone is connected through various means of communication, there is a constant flow of information, opinions, and even negativity. Social media platforms are filled with meticulously crafted highlight reels, presenting the best of people's lives, including their perfect vacations, beautifully decorated homes, and effortless achievements. This constant exposure to curated perfection fuels social comparison theory, which is the tendency to compare ourselves to others. As we are naturally inclined towards seeking dopamine, we often fall prey to the "Keeping Up With the Joneses" effect, a relentless pursuit to match or outdo what we perceive as others' success. This envy and mimetic desire can ultimately lead to feelings of inadequacy and dissatisfaction.

Focusing too much on individualism can lead to feelings of isolation and a lack of empathy. When we only care about projecting our own image, it becomes difficult to understand the struggles and complexities of others. Additionally, when we prioritize superficial charm and deception while being sensitive to criticism and seeking attention at all costs, we run the risk of developing the "dark triad" of personality traits (narcissism, Machiavellianism, and psychopathy) on a societal level. This erosion of empathy and ethical values can make it impossible to find happiness, enjoyment, and meaning in life.

Scapegoating has been used throughout history as a way for groups to shift the blame, often targeting a convenient victim, someone who is different from the majority, or someone who can be easily ostracized. This act serves a social function – it reduces anxiety, strengthens the group, and avoids deeper analysis of the root causes of the problem. Scapegoating may be a root cause of cancel culture's tendency to exclude people, but social media dynamics and the quest for online validation add a new layer. Cancel culture can be an effective tool for holding people accountable, but the potential for "victimhood chic" and the ease of online shaming require a more thoughtful approach. We must strive for a balance between calling out bad behavior and allowing for redemption while avoiding the pitfalls of mob mentality and mass shaming echo chambers.

The ease of communication online can breed a false sense of confidence, as described by the Dunning-Kruger Effect; people with limited knowledge overestimate their competence, leading to strong opinions and a lack of critical thinking. This, coupled with the anonymity and disinhibition that digital networks can provide, fosters a culture of outrage. Nuance and civil discourse get tossed aside as disagreements quickly snowball into online attacks.

Culture is an ever-changing phenomenon that has evolved over time. The norms, values, role models, and ways of the world are constantly in flux. It's important not to get caught up in temporary comparison traps and witch hunts. Instead, it's better to cultivate empathy and critical thinking. Before assigning blame, try to understand a

situation and work towards systemic change while holding individuals accountable for their actions. Remember,
actual progress isn't achieved by finding a scapegoat
but by addressing the root causes and collaborating
to create a better future. Genuine progress is achieved
through metacognition.

The Victimhood Chic

Mark Manson popularized the concept of 'victimhood chic,' which is a modern fallacy that explains how people tend to shift the responsibility of solving their own problems to others. We do this by blaming others, which provides us with a temporary sense of moral righteousness. This tendency is quite prevalent on social media, where people have an ingrained right to be outraged. The political left feels victimized by the right, American Ivy League students feel victimized by Israel for their actions towards Palestine, a middle-aged lady in San Francisco is offended by Christmas because it promotes capitalist spending rather than community spirit, the rich feel villainized from society, the poor feel succumbed to learned helplessness due to socioeconomic barriers, asylum seekers feel oppressed by their home state, and developed countries feel as though they have fallen victim to the effects of unemployment because of immigrants. It seems like every group has felt unfairly victimized by another, everywhere, all at once.

In the 21st century, the internet provided a medium for the decentralization of information, leading to the adoption of sensationalist media. In the past, we could curate our sources of information, with books and research being peer-reviewed and archived in libraries. News publications collectively worked to maintain a steady subscription base, creating a state of information symmetry for their readers. However, with the proliferation of social media and desensitization to conventional media, sensationalization has become the norm to garner attention. This has led to biased and opinionated storytelling, eroding trust in legacy media and fueling the adaptation of multi-source short format media consumption.

Although convenient, cordial, and candid, blitz information consumption is usually incomplete. This lack of complete information can lead to the 'Gell-Mann amnesia effect,' where we tend to be critical consumers of information in areas we understand, but gullible sponges in others. Our brains are wired for efficiency, and we develop mental shortcuts to trust certain sources for specific topics. In unfamiliar territory, our filters loosen, and we are more likely to be swayed by emotional appeal and dramatic presentation, especially in the bite-sized chunks of information offered by platforms like TikTok, YouTube, Twitter, and Facebook.

The 'Gell-Mann amnesia effect' can cause young and impressionable individuals to develop attitude inoculation. This theory explains how attitudes and beliefs can be made resistant to persuasion or influence. It can be applied to public campaigns that counter misinformation or spread fake news. Inoculating messages are designed to make the recipient feel threatened, which aids in recognizing the vulnerability of their current attitudes or beliefs. These messages also preemptively refute or defend against potential counterarguments. Unfortunately, this simplifies complex geopolitical and economic events into a "them vs. us" narrative, which often leads to outrage, polarization, and clickbait. To fully understand the situation, it is necessary to consider its historical context and competing interests, which require more effort. Therefore, nuance and complexities are often sacrificed for virality.

The worst part of this reality is that by being offended by everything, we strip attention away from real victims. We begin to acknowledge every minor inconvenience and infraction, devouring our time and mental capacity. This leads us to constantly sift through an array of hostile dissatisfactions, closing our eyes to the incredible things we do have. We must collectively prioritize showing gratitude, seeking the complete truth for the things that matter, and simply not policing almost everything the other 7+ billion people go through daily. Feeling like a victim will never leave you feeling happy, fulfilled, and satisfied with your current state.

The Werewolf Game

Game Instructions.

Number of Players: 8-12

Roles:

- Villagers (Majority): Try to identify and eliminate the werewolves.

- Werewolves (Minority): Work together to eliminate the villagers at night.

Gameplay:

i. **Introduction:** Roles are assigned secretly.

ii. **Daytime:** Players discuss the previous night's events, analyze behavior, and vote to eliminate one player they suspect.

iii. **Nighttime:** Werewolves secretly eliminate one villager.

iv. **Next Day:** Discussion and voting resume based on the previous night and the misinformation.

v. The game continues with night and day phases until all werewolves are eliminated (villagers win) or all villagers are eliminated (werewolves win).

Tips:

- Villagers: Pay close attention to details, voting patterns, alibis, and how players react to the misinformation. Look for inconsistencies and build a case based on logic and deduction.

- Werewolves: Coordinate your kills and use the misinformation to sow discord among the villagers. Don't be afraid to adapt your story based on the introduced twist.

Werewolf is a children's game, but it serves as a social deduction test where a hidden minority deceives an uninformed majority. In the game, villagers struggle to identify hidden werewolves who eliminate them during the night. This game draws a chilling parallel to real-world issues like misinformation and mob mentality, which have recurred throughout history. The werewolves exploit the villagers' limited information by demonstrating how informed they can be. Additionally, the game exposes the dangers of groupthink and mass hysteria. Groupthink is the tendency to prioritize group consensus over individual reasoning, while mass hysteria is a collective panic based on rumors or fear. In Werewolf, villagers with limited information rely on guesses and accusations. This fear and lack of logic fuel both groupthink and mass hysteria. Just as villagers fall for accusations in the game, real-world groups can be susceptible to manipulation by rumors and fear-mongering.

Werewolf isn't just fun; it's a reflection of human behavior. The game reveals how easily fear and suspicion can cloud judgment. It highlights the importance of critical thinking, especially when faced with limited information and social pressure. Confirmation bias occurs when we favor information that confirms our existing beliefs. Werewolf villagers exhibit this, as do people in online echo chambers. In the heat of the moment, emotions can overpower logic. By understanding these dynamics, we can become more critical thinkers and navigate the complexities of information in our own lives. The next time you encounter doubt or suspicion, remember the Werewolf within – a reminder to stay vigilant and think for yourself.

Social Constructivism

Social Constructivism is a theory in sociology that explains how knowledge is constructed. It suggests that our understanding of the world is not objective or pre-existing. Instead, it is an interpretation shaped by social interactions and cultural context. Our social interactions shape how we learn and make sense of the world through discussion, debate, and the sharing of experiences. Language is a tool we use to develop shared and meaningful understandings of the world. Our cultural backgrounds shape how we interpret information and experiences.

Knowledge is not universal; it varies across cultures. Our understanding of the world constantly evolves as we encounter new information and perspectives. Knowledge is dynamic and in constant flux with our current perceptions of objectivism, which posits that an objective reality exists independent of our perception or interpretation. Social Constructivism argues that even our understanding of the objective world is shaped by social factors.

Social Constructivism may seem confusing, but let me elaborate with real-world scenarios. Political science has defined the 'Coordination Problem' as: "A situation in which the interests of agents coincide, and the aim is to try to reach an outcome in which those interests are satisfied. A solution requires finding an equilibrium, meaning that no agent can do better by unilaterally doing something else, given the choices of the others." This concept is fundamental to understanding how societies function through language and social institutions as solutions to large-scale coordination problems.

Throughout human history, we have seen a mixture of cooperation, competition, and the development of shared beliefs. Yuval Noah Harari provides a detailed account of this journey, emphasizing how our societies were formed and how we have created objective realities through invention. From massive structures like pyramids to abstract concepts like money and nations, these are all products of our collective imagination.

One of the primary challenges faced by early human societies was the problem of coordination. Bands of hunter-gatherers living in scattered locations lacked the ability to organize large-scale projects. Social Constructivism helps us understand how shared beliefs and myths were used to bridge this gap. A unifying hero, like many prophets, martyrs, activists, leaders, and gods, serves as a prime example. Embellished and passed down through generations, legends transcended the boundaries of individual bands and fostered a sense of shared identity and purpose, enabling cooperation beyond the limitations of kinship.

Myth, as a social construct, empowered teamwork and laid the groundwork for complex societies. The pyramids of Egypt were not just feats of engineering; they were also powerful symbols of a unified state. The shared belief in their pharaohs' divinity and the afterlife, communicated through language, hieroglyphs, and rituals like mummification, served as social glue. This belief justified the immense effort required, directing individual actions towards the collective goal of glorifying the pharaoh and maintaining social order.

Social Constructivism emphasizes that imagined entities gain power if enough people believe in them. This concept underpins a range of human creations, from the seemingly mundane to the awe-inspiring. Money, for example, is a prime illustration. A decorated piece of paper has no inherent value. Its worth stems from a shared social agreement, a belief system we've collectively constructed. This belief enables trade, facilitates complex financial structures like banks and corporations, and powers novel creations like Bitcoin.

Similarly, governments are not natural phenomena. National borders and social security are human inventions established through cultural interaction, power dynamics, and shared narratives. As imagined entities, governments wield immense power because enough people believe in their legitimacy and authority. They establish laws and order, define ownership, and take preventative measures on behalf of the collective good of their citizens.

To a significant degree, concepts like class, culture, and social hierarchies are products of shared beliefs and narratives. They shape our perception/perspective of the world, dictate etiquette in societal interactions, and influence the decision-making of mutually exclusive individuals. By understanding how social realities are constructed, we gain the agency to challenge and potentially reshape them. Recognizing this empowers us to become active participants in determining our desires, values, and beliefs.

"With words, we make our world.
The stories we tell shape our reality."
- Michael Margolis.

CHAPTER 7

TULIP MANIA

During the mid-16th century, the Ottoman Empire introduced the tulip flower into the Dutch region. The tulip, which is a bulbous flower belonging to the lily family, became a symbol of wealth and affluence and gained popularity among noble houses and offices. In the 17th century, during the Dutch Golden Age, the price of tulips skyrocketed due to a surge in demand, reaching extraordinarily high rates. At one point, a single tulip bulb was valued at the same price as a house, and acquiring a tulip cost up to ten times the annual income of a white-collar worker. However, by 1634, the speculative bubble of the tulip bulb had reached its apex and dramatically collapsed three years later. This event, known as 'The Tulip Mania,' was the first recorded speculative/asset bubble in human history.

When the bubble burst, and market forces collectively decided that the intrinsic value of a tulip bulb was far too high, the immediate plummet in price left many investors in the asset financially vulnerable. It reinvented the invisible hand that controls the market forces of demand and supply. The tulip mania is a cautionary tale in the financial markets about speculation and the importance of informed financial decision-making.

The Luxury Trap

A Veblen good is a type of product where demand increases as the price goes up, which is the opposite of what happens in most cases. This occurs because these goods are perceived as exclusive and desirable status symbols. Therefore, Veblen goods exhibit an upward-sloping demand curve, unlike the typical downward-sloping curve. They are typically high-quality, highly coveted items that denote social status, such as luxury cars, yachts, fine wines, perfumes endorsed by celebrities, and designer jewelry.

DEMAND CURVE OF VEBLEN GOODS/SERVICES

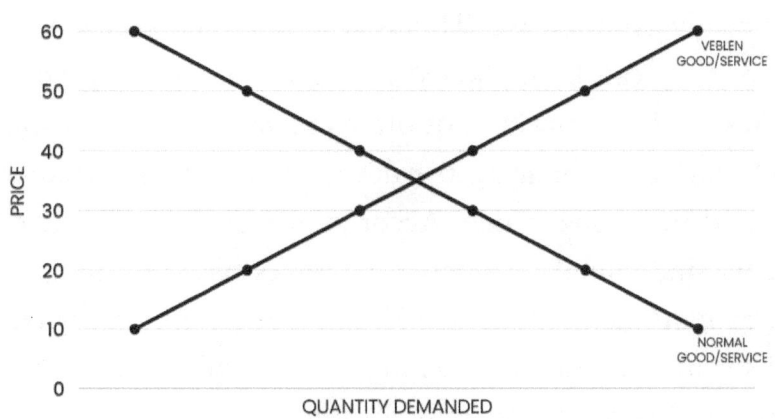

Economist Thorstein Veblen proposed that for some products, the high price itself becomes an attractive feature associated with exclusivity, status, and conspicuous consumption. These products tap into a fundamental human desire for recognition and social standing. Throughout history, philosophers have examined the concept of individual identity and how it relates to social structures. Conspicuous consumption, as demonstrated by pursuing Veblen goods, can signal membership in a particular social class. Sociologist Pierre Bourdieu argued that possessions serve as markers of distinction, indicating cultural capital and social position within a stratified society. Owning a Veblen good not only signifies one's wealth but also one's belonging in an exclusive group.

The idea of "perceived value" is a significant factor in how consumers view products. Often, people associate a higher price with better quality and exclusivity, even if this is not always the case. This is where Veblen goods come in, as they can be marketed to capitalize on this psychological bias. Luxury brands often create a sense of prestige and scarcity, enhancing the desirability of their products beyond functional value. According to social comparison theory, individuals evaluate themselves based on the people around them. Owning a Veblen good can fulfill a need for social validation and belonging, particularly in cultures that emphasize conspicuous consumption.

The allure of Veblen goods can lead to the "luxury trap," where people spend excessively in an attempt to gain status and social validation. Initially, people feel satisfied after acquiring a Veblen good, but this feeling can quickly fade as they feel the constant need to obtain the next status symbol as trends and social perception evolve. This constant urge to consume can lead to feelings of inadequacy and a distorted sense of self-worth tied solely to material possessions. Financially, the luxury trap can have significant consequences. The high costs of Veblen goods often lead to overspending, accumulating debt, and sacrificing other financial goals. This pattern can leave individuals financially vulnerable, especially during economic downturns.

To avoid falling into the luxury trap, it is crucial to develop intrinsic values that are not centered around material possessions. Focusing on personal development, establishing meaningful relationships, and gaining new experiences can lead to long-term fulfillment that does not depend on consumerism. Mindful consumption, involving critically assessing purchases and prioritizing needs over wants, is also helpful. Surrounding oneself with people who prioritize personal growth and experiences over conspicuous consumption can create a supportive environment for breaking free from the luxury trap.

Yuval Noah Harari's view on the Agricultural Revolution as a "luxury trap" provides an interesting insight into the relationship between Veblen goods and the societal implications of conspicuous consumption. It would be fascinating to examine how Harari's ideas intersect with the concepts we have previously discussed.

According to Harari, the transition from hunter-gatherer societies to agricultural ones was not a conscious decision aimed at achieving a better life. Instead, it was a gradual descent into a luxury trap. This concept aligns with Veblen goods, where initial improvements—such as the availability of wheat—led to benefits that required more investment of time and resources. The perceived benefits of agriculture, such as increased food security, obscured long-term costs. These included increased workload, generational immobility, the rise of social hierarchies and caste systems, unequal distribution of wealth, and shortened lifespans due to a less varied and lower-quality diet.

The "hedonic treadmill" concept states that accumulating wealth or resources does not necessarily lead to lasting happiness. This idea mirrors the psychology of the luxury trap, where an abundance of resources initially seems beneficial but ultimately leads to a cycle of toil without significant improvement in overall well-being. For example, in the case of agriculture, the abundance of wheat was initially seen as a great success in terms of food production. However, as dependence on agriculture grew, people had to work longer and harder to maintain production. What started out as a luxury of readily available food became a necessity, trapping people in relentless labor without significantly improving their overall quality of life.

While the success of increased food production led to a population boom in some societies, the individual cost of this success was immense. People traded their freedom, health, and leisure for a life of drudgery under oppressive regimes. This highlights a crucial limitation of economic models that focus solely on material progress without considering its impact on human well-being. Harari's concept suggests that the luxury trap extends beyond personal consumption. The abundance of food during the Agricultural Revolution led to the emergence of social classes, separating a ruling elite from a laboring peasantry. In a similar fashion, advanced societies today offer "luxuries" like legal systems and "wealth creation" that only benefit a privileged few. At the same time, the vast majority are trapped in a system that prioritizes societal advancement over individual well-being.

Even today, modern societies are grappling with the long-term consequences of the developmental ages that brought about previously non-existent issues such as social inequality, environmental degradation, and an incessant push for economic growth. Donald Trump is a poor person's idea of what a rich person would look like. When did private jets and heated floors in your toilet become the epitome of prosperity? Pop culture classics like 'American Psycho' and 'The Wolf of Wall Street' have become idealized versions of masculinity in adolescents. In our developmental years, we are generally addicted to video games and reality TV shows, stemming from our lack of career or purpose. The level-based ascension in video games or the advancing rounds of reality TV serve as proxies, substitutes for a missing sense of forward momentum, similar to adult obsession with sports, celebrities, or pornography. All proxies for community, fantasy, and physical intimacy that may be absent in their lives. The luxury trap gives away our power over ourselves for cheap dopamine in the form of indulgences and fallacies that mask harsh realities, potentially detracting from a life of fulfillment, enjoyment, and satisfaction. The luxury trap essentially flips Abraham Maslow's hierarchy of needs upside down, giving people a false sense of self-actualization and self-esteem, and redirecting humanity to chase physiological and social needs. By recognizing the possible dangers of the luxury trap, individuals and societies can make informed choices toward a future that values progress and human flourishing.

Social Charade

The act of gossiping is often deemed as insignificant chatter. However, if we delve deeper, we can unveil a fascinating interplay between our cognitive limits, social needs, and the very foundation of our societies. According to Robin Dunbar's Number theory, humans are restricted by cognitive limits, which permit us to maintain stable social relationships with a maximum of approximately 150 individuals. This theory aligns with the concept of constrained social networks explored in sociology, wherein our brains cannot handle the mental intricacies required to navigate complex webs of relationships exceeding this limit. In this context, gossip emerges as a crucial mechanism for social monitoring. By sharing information about the actions of others, individuals can stay informed about potential cheaters, free-riders, or those who violate social norms.

This aligns with Robert Trivers' theory of reciprocal altruism, which suggests that helping others with the expectation of receiving help in return is a common practice. This mutual exchange of benefits is often seen among social animals such as primates and birds. Gossip plays a crucial role in social enforcement by discouraging deviant behavior and promoting collaboration within the group.

In the early days of human civilization, gossip played a crucial role in maintaining social order and ensuring the group's survival. If someone were found to neglect their hunting duties or take more than their fair share of food, the group would talk about it, creating social pressure for the individual to conform to the group's expectations. It sounds a lot like evolutionary cancel culture, doesn't it? Our ability to share information about others beyond basic needs, such as food location, allowed us to form more extensive and cohesive communities than our Neanderthal cousins. By gossiping, we built coalitions and established complex social structures necessary for cooperative endeavors such as hunting large prey.

Gossip is not only limited to personal transgressions; it also includes discussions about objects, brands, and financial markets. This reflects how our natural gossiping tendencies have adapted to a more complex social and economic environment. Gossiping can be seen as a social bonding activity, as information sharing creates a sense of intimacy and trust among those involved. Laughter, shared secrets, and discussions about others can strengthen social bonds and build a sense of belonging.

However, it's important to recognize that gossip can be harmful and deceptive, spreading false information and damaging people's reputations. This behavior is often driven by a desire to elevate one's status within a group and exhibit biases against individuals within the same group. The sunk-cost fallacy from behavioral economics provides insight into this phenomenon. The tendency to persist with a failing course of action due to past invest-ment can be seen in gossip circles. For instance, imagine being loyal to a friend who constantly gossips negatively about others. Despite the discomfort, you might continue to engage in this behavior simply because you've already invested time and emotional energy in the friendship. This misplaced loyalty can lead to a vicious cycle of negativity.

From an evolutionary perspective, Dunbar suggests that gossip might be linked to kin selection, a concept ex-plored in sociobiology. This theory, championed by W.D. Hamilton, proposes that individuals are more likely to help close relatives due to shared genes. By sharing information about potential threats or opportunities, individuals can indirectly benefit their kin group.

Social networks are not just a group of people you know; they represent a form of social capital. Humans have a mental gauge that craves social acceptance and be-longing. This idea aligns with attachment theory, which highlights the critical role of social connection in healthy emotional development. For example, when starting a new job, having a solid network of colleagues can provide valuable information, mentorship opportunities, and emo-tional support, all of which can contribute to your suc-cess and well-being. Social capital works like a currency, providing access to resources, opportunities, and influence within a social system.

Social capital is not a static resource. Like financial capital, it needs constant investment and upkeep. If you fail to nurture your social network, it may eventually deteriorate. For example, if you don't cultivate relationships with your colleagues in your new job, those connections may weaken over time. This can negatively impact your access to valuable support and hinder your professional growth. Moreover, ideologies such as radical cancel culture or extreme political polarization can lead to social division and the breakdown of networks. Studies suggest that social exclusion triggers the same neural pathways as physical pain, highlighting the human aversion to being left out.

Gossip can impact social relationships in both positive and negative ways. It's essential to be self-aware and considerate when navigating social dynamics. Before spreading rumors or engaging in negative talk, consider the potential consequences and ask yourself if the information is necessary. Reflect on whether your intention is to build or destroy relationships. Remember that the power of gossip lies not just in the information shared but also in the purpose behind it. By harnessing the power of positive gossip and cultivating a network of supportive connections, you can create a more fulfilling and enriching life.

While social harmony is important, blind conformity can stifle progress. Individuals find a sense of belonging by aligning with groups that share their values. When used responsibly, gossip can actually help build and maintain positive social networks. Individuals tend to gossip selectively, focusing on information that strengthens social bonds and enhances reputations. For example, imagine gossiping with a friend about a colleague's recent act of generosity. This type of positive gossip can be a powerful way to nurture trust and cooperation within the workplace. Experiencing positive emotions broadens our attention and promotes social connection, making us more receptive to building positive relationships. This not only enhances your well-being but also opens doors to new friendships and strengthens your social network.

It's common for people to fear expressing their views when they differ from their friends who hold similar political beliefs. This fear of rejection can lead to self-censorship, especially among those with less education or social capital. People with higher levels of education may feel more empowered to challenge the status quo and express their viewpoints. Progress can only be made if people dare to challenge existing norms and propose alternative perspectives. If a scientific community discourages questioning established theories, it can stifle innovation and hinder progress. Similarly, challenging societal norms and proposing alternative viewpoints can lead to positive change in social spheres. For example, the Civil Rights Movement in the United States relied on the courage of individuals who challenged the status quo and advocated for racial equality.

While navigating social pressures can be challenging, it is important to balance harmony among a group and foster healthy debate. By cultivating self-awareness and critical thinking skills, you can engage in constructive conversations that challenge the status quo without resorting to negativity or personal attacks. Remember, true progress often stems from the courage to stand up for what you believe in, even when it's unpopular. In doing so, you can contribute to a more innovative and just society for all.

Perception is projection—a profound concept that empowers us to understand that what we perceive is a reflection of who we are. This understanding liberates us, as it reveals that we can only perceive what is already in our consciousness. As Swiss psychologist Carl Jung explained, we tend to project our most unconscious thoughts and emotions onto people and events around us. This means that we cannot perceive anything outside of ourselves that is not a part of us, giving us the power to shape our reality.

Gossip is a tool we use to create the world we want to experience and then project that world outside, making it the truth as we perceive it. Projection happens when we assign an element of our personality that resides in our unconscious to another individual or group. While we can project both positive and negative characteristics, we tend to project the negative ones more frequently. According to Sigmund Freud, who coined the term in the mid-1890s, projection is a defense mechanism used to avoid the anxiety that arises when one is forced to confront one's faults, weaknesses, and destructive tendencies. People often avoid acknowledging their faults and weaknesses by projecting them onto others. Our brains perpetuate our beliefs by recognizing the experiences that support them and blocking out anything that contradicts our worldview.

Every thought is a judgment, and the moment we pass judgment on someone or something, it becomes our perception, which is valid only for us. This realization inspires us to challenge our perceptions and consider alternative viewpoints. It is essential to remember that we always have a choice in our viewpoint. Instead of opting for the obvious interpretation of what we see, we can choose to look beyond it and consider if there is another perspective.

Paradox of Prosperity

Picture an unending dance on the savannah. A cheetah, a blur of muscle and grace, strains every ligament in pursuit of a gazelle, its swiftness honed by generations of relentless hunting. The gazelle, in turn, has evolved an uncanny ability to vanish into the tall grass. Its very existence depends on outsmarting its pursuer. This predator-prey dynamic is a fascinating display of co-evolution and offers a startling comparison to the self-destructive tendencies that lie within humanity.

Humans have long considered themselves the superior species on Earth, with a combination of intelligence and agility that allows them to dominate the planet. However, in this narrative, we often overlook the fact that we pose the greatest threat to our own long-term well-being. By examining our self-destructive tendencies through the lens of game theory, we can see that we are engaged in an "evolutionary game" against ourselves, constantly balancing between cooperation and self-destruction. This realization is sobering and highlights the need to take a more conscious and proactive approach toward our survival.

The prisoner's dilemma is a thought experiment in game theory. It involves two rational agents who have the option to cooperate with each other for mutual benefit or betray their partner for individual reward. In the typical prisoner's dilemma, both parties choose to protect themselves at the expense of the other participant, resulting in both being worse off than if they had cooperated.

HUMAN #1

GAME THEORY
THE PRISONER'S DILEMMA

HUMAN #2

	Cooperate	Don't Cooperate
Cooperate	**Mutual Gain** — Both players would receive a better payoff if they cooperated, but only if they trust each other.	**Diminished Return** — If one player cooperates and the other defects, the player that defects maximizes gain, and the player that cooperates will receive nothing.
Don't Cooperate	**Diminished Return** — If one player cooperates and the other defects, the player that defects maximizes gain, and the player that cooperates will receive nothing.	**Mutual Destruction** — If both players defect, they get a better payoff than they would have in the diminished return scenario.

The classic "prisoner's dilemma" perfectly encapsulates this internal struggle. Two individuals, faced with a choice to cooperate or betray, often end up worse off because each prioritizes immediate benefit over long-term mutual gain. This dilemma constantly plays out in our lives. Our 'predatory' instincts manifest as a relentless pursuit of immediate gratification. We crave sugary treats, succumb to the allure of risky shortcuts, and yearn for the fleeting validation of social media. These desires, like the cheetah's hunger, propel us towards short-term rewards, often at the expense of our long-term well-being. However, just as the gazelle embodies the 'prey' strategy, a powerful counterbalance exists within us. Our rational minds, driven by risk aversion and the desire for long-term security, strive for health, safety, and a sustainable environment. This 'prey' instinct compels us to make healthy choices, prioritize safety, and advocate for practices that ensure a thriving future for all.

The main issue in this internal conflict is the temptation of immediate gratification. Engaging in unhealthy habits brings a certain level of pleasure, much like a cheetah's satisfaction after a successful hunt. However, the consequences of self-destructive behavior often unfolds over time. The gradual effects of pollution, the negative impact on our health due to poor choices, and the unsustainable use of resources are easier to overlook because they happen slowly.

In addition, our personal behavior is heavily influenced by the choices made by those around us. If a significant portion of society prioritizes immediate gratification, it can create a social norm that promotes unhealthy behavior. The widespread availability of fast food, the constant exposure to social media that fuels envy and comparison, and the pressure to keep up with unrealistic lifestyles—all these factors make it difficult to resist the temptation to engage in detrimental activities.

The dynamics of predator and prey can be observed not only in individual behavior but also in human societies. Societies have developed various mechanisms to encourage cooperation. For example, gossip can be used as a form of "social disapproval" to discourage negative behaviors that harm the collective good. Cultural traditions and rituals often incorporate accumulated knowledge to avoid self-destructive practices passed down through generations. Like the cheetah refining its hunting tactics, our self-destructive tendencies can also become sophisticated. One example of this is scapegoating, where we deflect blame for our collective failures onto convenient targets. Similarly, the "luxury trap mentality" downplays the risks associated with unsustainable practices, enabling us to indulge in the short-term while ignoring the long-term consequences. The growing gap between the wealthy and the less wealthy is a consequence of the dilemma outlined above. When faced with a choice between promoting the common good or pursuing personal benefit, most people tend to choose the option that provides the greatest benefit for themselves, even if it comes at a cost to the majority. As a result, the overall loss for the masses increases, exacerbating the inequality further.

The struggle to resist destructive impulses is not an inevitable tragedy. We can emulate the resilience of the gazelle and devise strategies to outsmart our own 'predatory' instincts. The first step is acknowledging the internal conflict. It's important to recognize the appeal of short-term gratification and prioritize long-term well-being. Practices like mindfulness and self-reflection can help us become more aware of our inner dialogue. We must adjust our decision-making process to consider the long-term consequences of our choices instead of yielding to immediate temptation. Lastly, humans are social creatures. Surrounding ourselves with people who prioritize healthy habits and sustainable practices can create a powerful support system that fosters cooperation.

Advancements in technology have amazed us with the promise of a future beyond our wildest imaginations. However, there is an underlying feeling of unease that we may lose something essential in our relentless pursuit of progress. The solution to this problem lies not in the future but in our past history. Unlike any other species on Earth, humans have amassed a vast repository of knowledge over millennia. By learning from our ancestors' successes and mistakes, we can anticipate potential pitfalls and build upon previous accomplishments. This historical context is what distinguishes us and elevates us. This knowledge is not solely stored in libraries and databases but is also passed down through generations within our communities. However, as our communities evolve and virtual spaces rise, our interactions are becoming increasingly limited. This, according to the separation theory, leads to weakened communities. The nuclear family is often the last refuge of personal connections to our history and plays a crucial role in passing down accumulated knowledge. It nurtures a sense of belonging and provides a safety net that allows individuals to explore the world and take risks. Strong family units create a foundation for healthy coping mechanisms, thereby reducing self-destructive behaviors.

Have you ever wondered why some of the wealthiest and most successful societies are still struggling with various issues? It's a paradox: prosperous cultures filled with opportunities, yet plagued by self-destructive behaviors. The answer lies in the complex interplay between human psychology and social systems. Imagine a flourishing community where everyone is busy chasing the next big thing. According to social disorganization theory, social bonds weaken during times of prosperity, giving way to a focus on material possessions and individual goals. As materialism and individualism take center stage, the ties that once bound individuals together may begin to fray. Norms lose their guiding influence, and individuals may find themselves adrift, seeking comfort in self-destructive behaviors as a coping mechanism to deal with their sense of isolation. People tend to feel left behind, even when things seem good. We often compare ourselves to others, and during times of abundance, the gap between those who have it all and those who don't can widen. This frustration can fuel self-destruction, as some may lash out or lose hope in the face of perceived injustice. Relative deprivation theory explains how perceptions of well-being are not determined by absolute wealth but by comparisons to others.

When we feel stagnant and stuck in life, we often fail to understand that it's not because the world around us is moving too fast and leaving us behind. Instead, our innate need for constant growth exacerbates this notion. This often leads to an existential crisis, subconsciously encouraging us to disrupt our lives, enabled by a culture of victimhood that lets us blame circumstances for our lack of progress. The remedy for this is having something to look forward to in the future. However, this is a double-edged sword; the value you seek from the future must positively contribute to your overall well-being, requiring you to forgo instant gratification for meaningful gain. This fundamental need is best fulfilled by changing your routine through self-improvement, which generates a sense of empowerment and forward momentum.

Hedonic adaptation explains why people living in developed societies quickly adjust to positive environmental changes and lose their initial pleasure and satisfaction. This phenomenon leads individuals to engage in risky or self-destructive behaviors to recapture fleeting moments of euphoria. However, they often fail to realize that their actions only perpetuate a cycle of dissatisfaction and longing. Imagine being presented with countless options to choose from. It can be overwhelming and lead to impulsive decision-making. This unchecked abundance can cause individuals to sacrifice long-term goals for instant gratification. It is crucial to recognize the adverse effects of excess choice and actively make thoughtful, intentional decisions that align with our overall goals and values. The Easterlin paradox suggests that wealth and economic prosperity do not always lead to happiness. Individuals may feel unhappy if they cannot match their peers' social or financial status despite having material possessions. This paradox highlights that material possessions alone cannot guarantee lasting happiness. Humans naturally compete with each other, which can manifest in ways like sabotaging their potential to avoid feeling outdone or causing harm to others. The "us vs. them" mentality is deeply rooted in our evolutionary past and can lead to feelings of superiority and invincibility, eventually leading to our downfall.

You could be on the trip of your life but still feel a sense of dread because, deep down, you fear that you aren't where you'd like to be in the grand vision of your future. You could be surrounded by the best people yet still have self-debilitating anxiety that prevents meaningful conversations because you're worried about passing judgment and missing opportunities. The first few years of life are usually blissful. The young, oblivious child enjoys a world that has no evil. But as you get older and more aware, life becomes more complicated. As time passes, we lose control over our own lives and surroundings, and we become better at compartmentalizing within the boundaries of delusion we set for ourselves. And that's okay; after all, we must do what is necessary to remain unbroken. As we mature and age, we are far less proficient at managing our emotions. The grief of the past deepens, and the anxiety of future challenges compound in delayed reactions as we distract and suppress our feelings with possessions, geographical escapes, and endless scrolling. Yes, it is imperative to have fun as you navigate through chaos, but at some point, you must stop and clean up the messes you've been avoiding. Because in life, there is always so much going on around you that you don't even realize.

The paradox of thriving cultures is a call to action; amidst this self-destructive behavior, I would like to preach a message of hope and reassure everyone that we can mitigate our collective demise. However, the reality is that there is no hope for us. We are powerless to stop our cyclical nature from tearing down what we build and replacing it with something better. The only permanent facet of our reality is impermanence—constant change in the name of evolution. That is the way of humanity. Matriphagy, a word as unsettling as the act it describes, is the consumption of a mother by her offspring. In some corners of the animal kingdom, it's a brutal necessity. Spiderlings devour their silk-spinning mother, inheriting the very substance that gave them life. This shocking image can be seen as a metaphor for a dark undercurrent in human history. We also struggle with a kind of matriphagy, a yearning to tear down the old world order, the "mother" that nurtured us, in hopes of building something better. The cyclical rise and fall of civilizations reflect this. Like the spiderlings, will we destroy the very systems that gave us life in a desperate bid for progress?

CHAPTER 8

FALLEN EMPIRES

The Prophecy

As an academic, I was taught to expect recessions, a crisis, or a period of negative growth in the economy, life, and the world. While I didn't anticipate a global pandemic, I knew something was coming. From the dot-com bubble before I was born, the 9/11 attack the day after I was born, the 2008 financial crisis at the age of seven, to the COVID-19 lockdowns during my senior year of high school, I've been trying to understand why we constantly face turmoil that worsens our lives. Most often, these crises are due to our own actions.

Recently, I came across the theory of the 'Fourth Turning' by Neil Howe and William Strauss. The book provides a mind-blowing analysis of how and when history repeats itself. According to the book, history repeats itself in 80-year blocks called "speculums," which we can refer to as 'history blocks'. These blocks aren't exactly 80 years long—this is history, not math—but they roughly span a human lifetime, typically 80 to 90 years. Within these 80-year history blocks, there are four turnings of about 20 years each. We usually call them generations, but the book refers to them as 'turnings.' Turnings are similar to seasons, like spring, summer, fall, and winter. Throughout our history, we've had these 80-year blocks, which have been remarkably similar to one another.

We live in a historical cycle known as a 'turning,' divided into four parts or seasons, each with a distinct mood and energy. The first turning is a time of vibrant optimism and deep unity, where people experience a sense of promise and belonging. However, societal norms and expectations are highly valued, creating a culture of shame. Public discourse revolves around the means to achieve goals rather than the goals themselves, and action is prioritized over emotion. Middle-aged individuals hold significant political power, gender differences are more pronounced, and parenting is less protective compared to previous eras. Social demand for order peaks as political order increases, leading to the decay of old values and the establishment of a new civic order.

The second turning is a time of questioning and rebellion, marked by euphoria and defiance. Guilt rises as people become more aware of their past actions and seek to avoid shame. Individuals are elevated, and private spaces are reinvented. The cultural calendar resets, and gender distinctions begin to narrow. Parenting becomes more underprotective, and a new values regime will challenge the civic order. As the political supply of order peaks, the social demand for order will fall.

The third turning is a time of uncertainty and unraveling. During this epoch, people feel separated and anxious, with guilt at an all-time high. Individuality is highly valued, and public debates focus on the end goal rather than the means to achieve it. Society is empathetic and capable of feeling but lacks the ability to act.

The fourth and final turning is a time of crisis and upheaval, which mostly focuses on survival and gathering. People feel a sense of shame as they regret their past actions and try to avoid guilt. Group mentality is highly rewarded and prompted, whereas the public space is reinvented, and the political calendar is reset. Gender distinctions increase, and overprotective parenting is widespread. As the political supply of order reaches its lowest point, the social demand for order increases. Unfortunately, at the time of writing, in 2024, we are in the fourth turning, which means we are experiencing a period of great turmoil and change.

1st Turning - High
Era of promise, belonging.

Sense of shame reaches zenith; duty, conformity rewarded.

Public debate over means, not ends.
Society can *do*, but not *feel*.

Mid-lifers powerful in politics.

Gender distinctions are widest.

LESS PROTECTIVE parenting.

2nd Turning - Awakening
Era of euphoria, defiance.

Sense of guilt rises; people guilty about what they did to avoid shame.

Individual elevated.

Private space reinvented.
Cultural calendar reset.

Gender distinctions narrow.

UNDERPROTECTIVE parenting.

Social demand for order peaks as political supply of order rises.

Old values regime decays; new civic order implants.

Civic order attacked by new values regime.

Social demand for order falls as political supply of order peaks.

SPRING
growth, childhood

SUMMER
jubilation, youth

WINTER
death, old age

AUTUMN
fragmentaion, mid-life

Social demand for order rises as political supply of order reaches nadir.

New values regime propels transformation of civic order.

Civic order decays; new values regime implants.

Social demand for order reaches nadir as political supply of order falls.

4th Turning - Crisis
Era of survival, gathering.

Sense of shame rises; people ashamed about what they did to avoid guilt.

Group elevated.

Public space reinvented.
Political calendar reset.

Gender distinctions widen.

OVERPROTECTIVE parenting.

3rd Turning - Unraveling
Era of separation, anxiety.

Sense of guilt reaches zenith; principle, individuality rewarded.

Public debate over ends, not means.
Society can *feel*, but not *do*.

Mid-lifers powerful in culture.

Gender distinctions are narrowest.

MORE PROTECTIVE parenting.

By Steve Barrera (sbarrera@mindspring.com), adapted from *The Fourth Turning*, William Stauss and Neil Howe, 1997, Broadway Books.

Let's look closer at our history, specifically the period after America's victory in World War II. This period is referred to as the 'high' and is marked by an even distribution of wealth. During this time, the average person could work at a gas station and still afford to buy a house. It was a time of cultural and technological advancement, with the birth of rock and roll and achievements such as launching monkeys and men into space. The 'high' ended with the assassination of John F. Kennedy on November 22, 1963. However, it is essential to note that this period was not a 'high' for everyone.

During this period in America, the South was segregated, homosexuality was illegal and was considered a mental disorder, and there was a strong emphasis on conformity. However, the Age of Non-conformity and Social Justice started during the Awakening period. This era was characterized by passion and saw the rise of Martin Luther King and the Civil Rights Movement, as well as protests against the Vietnam War, the Women's Liberation Movement, and the Gay Rights Movement. It was also a time of great movies, fantastic music, and technological advancements, such as the debut of the first Macintosh computer and the birth of Apple Inc. The Awakening period was marked by an increasing emphasis on individualism and ended with the re-election of Ronald Reagan in 1984.

During the third turning, chaos prevailed. The fall of Soviet communism marked the beginning of the Russian gangster state and resulted in an unraveling of societal norms. Meanwhile, musicians sang about violence and decay in their deteriorating cities. Concurrently, the LA riots, O.J. Simpson's trial, the 9/11 attacks, and wars in Afghanistan and Iraq further contributed to societal decline. The unraveling ultimately culminated in the financial crisis of 2008. Interestingly, the book that predicted the current fourth turning was written during the last third turning and published in 1997.

'The Fourth Turning' suggests that every 80 years, there is a significant crisis in America and the other grand institutions of the world. The last fourth turning took place 80 years ago, leading to the Great Depression and World War II. Before that, the Civil War marked a fourth turning, and even before that was the Revolutionary War. We are currently amid the latest fourth turning, and it is up to us to save the world. Where do you fit into all of this, and what is your role?

Each generation tends to embody a specific archetype based on when they were born. This archetype defines the generation in its prime and midlife, which will shape society towards the next high. The boomer archetype is the prophet—Bill Gates and Steve Jobs are boomers and prophets who predicted that one day, not only big corporations and governments, but everyone would own a computer. Gates even predicted a crisis like COVID-19 five years before it happened. The authors of this book also belong to the boomer generation and share this prophetic mindset. Gen X is characterized as the nomad generation, consisting of travelers with no fixed home, explorers, migrants, and pioneers of globalization.

The book suggests that millennials, raised during a time of great upheaval, will eventually be recognized as the hero generation. In today's world, individuals such as Barack Obama, frontline hospital workers, and Malala Yousafzai exemplify this heroism. It is predicted that millennials will parallel the World War II heroes of past generations. As for Generation Z, their talents are yet to be fully realized, but they are predicted to be an artist generation. From this group, we can expect to see the emergence of the next Bill Withers, Toni Morrison, or Bob Dylan—all born during times of crisis and belonging to an artistically transformative generation.

The historical period before ours concluded with World War II and commenced with the Civil War 80 years prior. The history block before that concluded with the Civil War and started with the end of the Revolutionary War. Similarly, we are now at the end of our history block, right in the middle of a crisis, and are currently changing our world again.

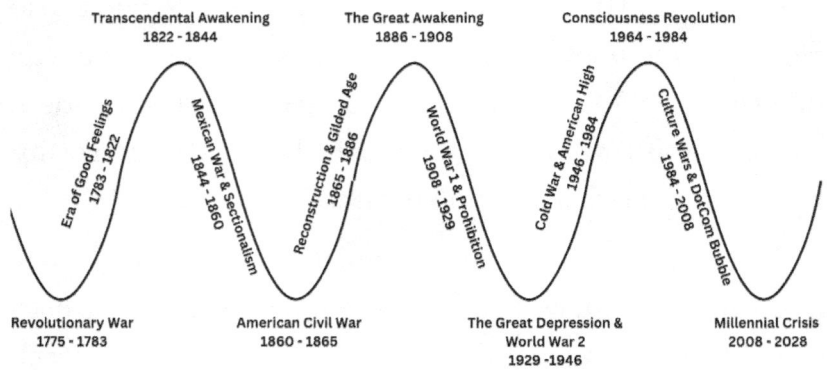

'The Fourth Turning' suggests that crises are unpleasant yet necessary, shifting the balance of power from the older generation to the younger. However, this victory is not certain, and each of us must step up during this difficult time. We must work to strengthen our positive qualities as we strive for a better future. In fact, our modern society was designed to encourage the potential of every individual, and it is the collective efforts of individuals that keep it thriving.

What could be your role in helping to resolve the crisis? My generation, Gen Z, is responsible for repairing and rebuilding the mess left by others. Our purpose is to clean, fix, and reimagine the world for the better. We were born into the digital era, the first of the hyperconnected world, and we have a particular knack for reinventing the wheel.

Perhaps our nomadic generation is tasked with ferrying society from one historical cycle (speculum) to another.

But where do we start? Begin by focusing on yourself, then the five people closest to you, followed by your nuclear family, your community, and finally, the world. You are burdened with the glorious purpose of dreaming up a new world. For the next 80 years, the following four generations—the successive fourth turnings—depend on the foundation we build long after we are but fragmented memories and specks of dirt.

The Death of Kings

> *"The past isn't real. It's a story we tell ourselves.*
> *History, in the wrong hands, is the most*
> *dangerous tool ever invented. History isn't fact.*
> *It's a narrative, one carefully curated and shaped.*
> *Under the right scribe, a hero becomes a villain,*
> *a victory becomes a tragedy, and a lie becomes*
> *the truth. The storyteller controls the narrative.*
> *History is written by the victors, but it is rewrit-*
> *ten by those who seek the truth."*
> *- The Foundation Trilogy.*

Raymond Thomas Dalio is the founder and manager of one of the most prestigious hedge funds in the United States, with over 50 years of experience in global macro-economic investing. Renowned as an enthusiastic student of historical pattern recognition, Dalio explores the last 500 years of history and identifies recurring situations in his book—The Changing World Order. In chaos theory, the butterfly effect challenges predictability, highlighting the profound interconnectedness of our world where even seemingly minor events can trigger vast repercussions. The butterfly effect invites the modern world to find beauty in the unpredictable, acknowledging its infinite potential to shape our destinies within its delicate flutter. Contrasting this viewpoint, however, Dalio and the authors of 'The Fourth Turning' align with deterministic theory—which rejects chaos. This philosophical concept suggests that all events, including human actions, are determined by preceding causes or natural laws. It asserts that knowing the exact state of a system at a particular time allows for precise predictions of its future state, implying that all events unfold along predetermined paths without randomness or free will.

So, where exactly do we fit into these theories? Do we have complete autonomy over our actions, which may potentially lead to global implications? Or are we merely cogs in the extensive systems we have created to solve our coordination problems for a better tomorrow?

Ray Dalio's analysis of the natural hegemons that rose over the last five centuries, including the Dutch, British, and US empires, reveals a perpetually changing world order. In 1971, when Dalio was a young clerk on the New York Stock Exchange floor, the United States ran out of money and defaulted on its debts. This happened because, back then, gold was the currency used in international transactions. Paper money, like the dollar, was similar to checks in a checkbook and had no intrinsic value beyond its ability to be exchanged for gold, which was considered real money.

At the time, the United States was spending a lot more money than it was earning, printing more paper money than it had gold reserves to back it up. As people started exchanging their paper money for gold, the US gold reserves began to dwindle. It was soon evident that the United States could not meet its obligations to exchange all the paper currency in circulation for gold. Consequently, holders of dollars rushed to exchange them for gold before the US gold reserves were depleted. President Nixon addressed the nation on a television appearance on August 15th, 1971, announcing that the US would no longer allow individuals to exchange their dollars for gold without indicating that the country was defaulting. This marked the end of the mid-1900s.

What a crisis! Dalio expected the stock market to collapse the next day. However, when the opening bell rang, chaos ensued, albeit not the expected kind. Instead of plummeting, the stock market skyrocketed and rose to nearly 25%. This outcome surprised all observers. Upon further investigation, Dalio discovered that a similar event had occurred in 1933, which had the same effect. Back then, paper dollars were backed by gold, but the US was depleting its gold reserves due to excessive spending. President Roosevelt, the White House resident then, publicly announced the decision to abandon the country's promise to exchange dollars for gold.

In both instances, 1933 and 1971, breaking the link to gold allowed the US to sustain its deficit spending by simply printing more paper money. As the number of dollars increased without any corresponding increase in the country's wealth, the value of each dollar decreased. These new dollars entered the market without boosting productivity, leading to increased prices of stocks, gold, and commodities because they were also used to purchase the aforementioned. This same phenomenon was a recurring pattern in the global economy.

Throughout history, governments, dictators, kings, and dynastic empires have consistently spent more than they earned from taxes, leading to financial crises and the need for more funds. To address these deficits, they often resorted to printing more money, which caused its value to fall and led to a rise in the prices of commodities, gold, and stocks. This was when Dalio first understood the principle that when central banks print money to deal with a crisis, it's a good idea to invest in commodities, gold, and stocks because they will increase in value while paper money will lose its value. This printing of money occurred during the mortgage-driven debt crisis in 2008 and the pandemic-driven economic crisis of 2020. It is likely to happen again in the future. The key lesson here is that understanding historical precedents is essential for anticipating future economic conditions and navigating them effectively.

In 2020, the global pandemic caused financial difficulties for many countries trying to pay off their debts. Even after reducing interest rates to zero, they were unable to meet their obligations. As a result, central banks resorted to printing more money, leading to growing wealth and value gaps. These gaps triggered conflicts within societies, leading to political populism and polarization between the left, who seek to redistribute wealth, and the right, who want to protect those who possess wealth. One of the most noticeable manifestations of societal distress is the resurgence of identity politics. As economic conditions worsen, the focus shifts from fiscal policies to questions of identity, cultural narratives, and belonging. This has caused people to seek comfort and solidarity in their identities based on ethnicity, sexuality, religion, or ideology, further dividing society and polarizing public discourse. Moreover, conflicts between rising powers and leading powers have been escalating, adding to the challenges faced by the world.

Let's reflect on the past. The sequence of events we are currently experiencing has happened many times before, and it usually leads to changes in domestic and world orders. We last saw this from 1930 to 1945. But what exactly is an order? An order is a system of governance that regulates interactions between individuals or groups of people. Internal orders govern within countries, usually outlined in constitutions, while world orders govern interactions between countries, typically outlined in treaties. Internal and world orders change at different times, but they usually shift after wars—whether civil wars within countries or international wars between nations. New revolutionary forces overthrow old, weak orders, leading to new governing systems. The United States Constitution was established in 1789 following the American Revolution and continues to be the governing law today, despite the American Civil War. Similarly, Russia underwent a significant transformation with the Russian Revolution in 1917, which ended peacefully in 1991. China also experienced substantial changes following the victory of the Chinese Communist Party in the civil war of 1949, which led to the establishment of the current internal order. The current world order, also known as the American world order, emerged after the Allied victory in World War II, with the US becoming the dominant world power. Thereby, agreements and treaties were drawn up to regulate global governance and monetary systems.

The Bretton Woods Agreement of 1944 established the US dollar as the world's leading reserve currency, marking the start of a new world order. Over the past 500 years, several empires and their reserve currencies have risen and declined, including the Dutch Empire and the guilder, the British Empire and the pound, and the US Empire and the dollar. The Chinese empire has also gone through cycles of decline and resurgence. Other notable empires, such as the Spanish, German, French, Indian, Japanese, Russian, and Ottoman Empires, have also experienced significant conflicts and cycles of rise and decline.

Empires have experienced a repeated sequence of rise and fall in overlapping cycles that lasted around 250 years. These cycles were separated by transition periods lasting between 10 to 20 years. Typically, these transition periods have been times of great conflict; leading powers only fall with a fight. We can simplify the concept of the rise and decline of a typical empire by focusing on the pattern of cause-effect relationships. Generally, better education leads to increased innovation and technology development. This, in turn, results in the establishment of the currency as a reserve currency. The major cycle typically begins after a significant conflict, such as a war, establishes a new leading power and world order. As this power is not challenged, peace and prosperity usually ensue. As people become more familiar with this prosperous and peaceful time, they depend more on it continuing. To do so, they borrow money, which leads to a financial bubble. The share of trade of the leading power increases, and as most transactions occur in its currency, it becomes a reserve currency and encourages further borrowing. However, this increased prosperity results in an unequal distribution of wealth, causing the wealth gap to widen between the rich "haves" and the poor "have-nots."

Over time, financial bubbles tend to burst, leading to an increase in internal conflict between the rich and the poor. This conflict can lead to a peaceful redistribution of wealth or result in a civil war. As the empire struggles with this internal conflict, its power diminishes relative to rising external powers. The latest winners and losers emerge when a new power becomes strong enough to compete with the dominant power experiencing domestic breakdowns, external conflicts, and wars. These winners unite to create a new world order, and the cycle begins again. Like human life cycles, no two are identical, but most are similar. They're driven by logical relationships that progress through stages from birth to strength, maturity, weakness, and inevitably decline.

Age alone cannot determine a person's or empire's lifespan. It is vital to keep track of the critical power indicators to predict what might happen in the future. Generally, this cycle has three phases: the rise, top, and decline. A successful new order that rises internally and externally is usually initiated by influential revolutionary leaders who do four things:

1. To win power, they gain more support than the opposition. Their strategy to consolidate power involves either converting, weakening, or eliminating any opposition to ensure no obstacles stand in their way.

2. They establish institutions and systems that function well to make the country work efficiently.

3. They choose their successors wisely or create systems that do so because a great empire requires many great leaders over several generations.

THE CHANGING WORLD ORDER

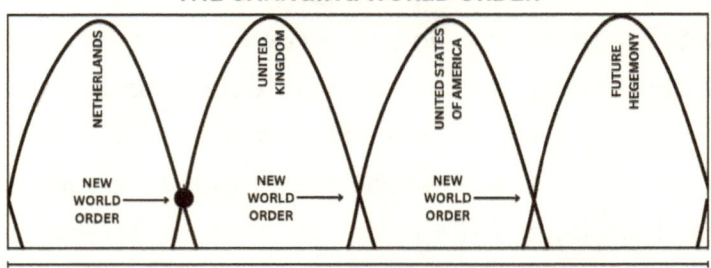

After winning a battle, the country usually goes through a peaceful and prosperous period where the leadership is dominant and has support from the people—the first turning. Leaders create an excellent system to increase the country's wealth and power. A robust education is crucial for achieving greatness, as it would impart knowledge and inculcate strong character, civility, and work ethic. It is essential to impart these values within families, schools, and religious institutions so that individuals can learn to respect rules and laws, maintain social order, reduce corruption, and work together towards a shared goal. As the country progresses, it should shift from producing essential products to innovating and inventing new technologies. For example, the Dutch defeated the Habsburg Empire and achieved superb education, becoming so inventive that they invented a quarter of all major inventions worldwide. Their most significant invention was ships that could travel around the world. Similarly, the United States established universities and knowledge hubs like Silicon

Valley, leading to innovations like social media, artificial intelligence, and autonomous driving.

A cycle of income growth can be used to fund investments in education, infrastructure, and research and development. Successful empires have used a capitalist approach to develop productive entrepreneurs. A reserve currency enables an empire to borrow more than other countries, which is a huge advantage. As people in rich and powerful countries earn more, they become less competitive than those in other countries who work for less. As people accumulate wealth, they often work less, indulge in leisure activities, and pursue more refined and less productive endeavors. Over time, this can lead to decadence. Values tend to shift as generations pass, and wealth and power are inherited rather than earned through hard work. The next generation may lack the experience of overcoming challenges, being used to luxury and accustomed to a more leisurely lifestyle. This makes them more vulnerable to facing difficulties and obstacles.

During the Victorian era, the British Empire experienced a period of high prosperity. As people became accustomed to doing well, they began to bet on the good times, continuing by borrowing money, eventually leading to financial bubbles. Naturally, not everyone benefited equally from these economic gains, causing the wealth gap to widen. Wealth gaps are self-reinforcing because wealthy individuals use their significant resources to maintain power and influence. For example, they can give their children a better education and influence the political system to their advantage. This results in growing differences in values, politics, and opportunities between the wealthy "haves" and the poor "have-nots." Those who are less well-off may feel that the system is unfair, leading to resentment. However, as long as the living standards of most people continue to rise, these resentments do not boil over into conflict.

As the world's reserve currency, countries tend to borrow excessively, accumulating large debts with foreign lenders. This boosts spending power in the short term but weakens the country's financial health and currency in the long term. National power is maintained through borrowing, funding excessive domestic consumption, and international military conflicts essential for preserving the empire. However, the cost of maintaining and defending the empire eventually surpasses its revenue, making the empire unprofitable.

Since September 11th, the United States has spent roughly 8 trillion dollars on foreign wars and their aftermaths, in addition to trillions more on various military operations and the maintenance of military bases. Richer countries borrow from poorer countries, which save more, leading to a shift in wealth and power. When the empire runs out of new lenders, those holding the currency begin to sell and exit rather than buy, save, lend, and invest.

As a result, the empire's strength declined gradually and suddenly due to internal economic weakness and internal conflict. When debts become very large, the empire may no longer be able to borrow the necessary funds to repay them, leading to a financial bubble burst. The nation then faces a difficult decision between defaulting on its debt obligations or devaluing its currency and increasing inflation, creating significant domestic hardships.

When the government struggles to fund itself, and the economy is in a bad state, living standards decline, and the gaps between wealth, values, and politics widen. This results in increased internal conflict between groups, such as the rich and the poor, as well as various ethnic, religious, and racial groups. This unraveling is typically marked by the 'third turning,' leading to political extremism on either the left or the right. On the left, there are attempts to redistribute wealth, while on the right, the goal is to keep the wealth concentrated among the rich. During these times, taxes on the wealthy usually increase. When the rich feel their wealth and well-being are at risk, they may move their assets, currencies, and even themselves to safer places. This outflow of wealth reduces the empire's tax revenue, creating a self-reinforcing, hollowing-out process. If the outflow becomes severe, governments may ban it, causing panic among those trying to protect their assets.

Turbulent conditions can reduce economic growth, leading to conflicts over resource allocation and the emergence of leaders who promise to restore order. This can challenge democracy, leading to the rise of a robust populist leader. Internal conflict can escalate into revolution or civil war, resulting in peaceful or violent changes in the existing order. This weakens the empire, making it vulnerable to external rivals and leading to significant international conflicts that require increased military spending. Without a workable process for resolving international disputes peacefully, such conflicts are typically settled through displays of power. The leading empire must choose between fighting or retreating, both of which have negative consequences. Poor economic conditions often lead to disputes over wealth and power, ultimately resulting in war—known as the 'fourth turning.'

Wars are expensive, but they often bring about significant changes that shift the balance of power and wealth. The end of a declining empire's cycle typically occurs when those holding its reserve currency and debt lose faith and begin selling it. Of approximately 750 currencies used since 1700, less than 20% still exist, and all have been devalued. For example, the Dutch sell-off led to a currency devaluation, while the British sell-off led to the establishment of a new world order.

Despite the United States' huge debt and deficits funded by borrowing and printing new money, the country has not yet reached this point. While conflicts occur, they have not yet escalated into wars. Eventually, new winners emerge from these conflicts, regardless of whether they are violent or not. These winners unite to restructure the losers' debts and political systems, establishing a new world order. This process marks the end of the old cycle and empire and the beginning of the new one. The cycle then repeats itself.

"Where are we heading?" — This is a common question we ask ourselves, especially when we consider the fate of empires. Most empires go through a cycle of prosperity and decline, and specific indicators can help us predict which stage an empire is in, how healthy it is, and whether it is improving or worsening. In many cases, a nation's most prominent internal challenge stems from its ability to make the tough decisions necessary for long-term success. With all this in mind, let me circle back to my initial question. Are we part of the deterministic theory that asserts randomness or free will to be inconsequential in unfolding events, as everything follows a predetermined path based on prior conditions? Or is chaos theory right, preaching the release of our illusion of control and finding beauty in the unpredictable?

"The pattern of history is never linear;
it is a tapestry of interconnected events."
- The Foundation Trilogy.

The concept of deterministic chaos refers to a type of behavior that occurs when a system adheres to a set of deterministic rules. If you know the starting conditions and the rules, you can predict the system's behavior with certainty. Despite this, the system exhibits chaotic behavior due to its complexity. Even small changes in the initial conditions or inputs can lead to significantly different outcomes. Interestingly, there is no randomness or probability involved in these rules. However, as the rules are applied repeatedly, the system's behavior becomes incredibly complex and unpredictable. This complexity results from the interactions among the system's components and the feedback loops. Thus, deterministic chaos is about systems that, despite following simple deterministic rules, exhibit behavior that appears random and unpredictable over time due to their complex interactions.

The only way to break the cyclical nature of the turnings, the changing orders, the curse of consciousness, and humanity's pathological tendency to unknowingly perpetuate their own downfall, is by creating system complexities with a functional feedback loop. Functional feedback loops, without the effects of cancel culture, scapegoating, and mimetic rivalry, diminish its impact. Actual change isn't made through extreme radicalism and bigotry; instead, true progress is made by adopting a metacognitive outlook on every facet of your existence.

"Violence is the last refuge of the incompetent. Any dogma, based primarily on faith and emotionalism, is a dangerous weapon to use on others since it is almost impossible to guarantee that the weapon will never be turned on the user. The fall of the empire is a massive thing, however, and not easily fought. It is dictated by a rising bureaucracy, a receding initiative, a freezing of caste, a damming of curiosity—a hundred other factors. It has been going on for centuries and is too majestic and massive a movement to stop. Any fool can tell a crisis when it arrives. The real service to the state is to detect it in the embryo."

- The Foundation Trilogy.

An Inconsequential Life

The "Universe 25" experiment was conducted in the 1960s by American psychologist John B. Calhoun. The aim of this experiment was to observe the impact of population density on behavior, reproduction, and mortality in a population of mice. The experiment took place in a specially designed enclosure called Universe 25, which was a large, climate-controlled space with abundant food, water, and nesting materials provided. The study focused on the effects of abundance and the social dynamics of overcrowded populations.

Universe 25, at its inception, held the promise of a utopia. A spacious enclosure brimming with all the comforts a mouse could desire food in abundance, water glistening like liquid silver, and soft nesting materials aplenty. Into this idyllic haven, a handful of mice were introduced, their numbers small, their potential vast, allowing them to breed freely. Initially, the population increased as the mice had access to ample resources and space. As time went on its relentless march, so too did the population of Universe 25. What had once been a tranquil haven soon transformed into a bustling metropolis of fur and whiskers. With each passing day, the once plentiful resources dwindled, giving rise to a new reality—a reality of scarcity and competition. As the population increased, space became limited, leading to overcrowding. Mice began to compete for resources such as food, water, and nesting sites. With increasing population density, social hierarchies among the mice began to break down. Aggressive behaviors, such as territoriality, increased as individuals competed for limited resources. As overcrowding persisted, Calhoun observed the emergence of abnormal behaviors among the mice. Some individuals became isolated, while others exhibited repetitive behaviors or violence towards each other.

The social fabric began to fray in the gray corners of Universe 25. In the past, there was a strong sense of friendship and mutual trust among the group, but now there is a growing feeling of dissatisfaction and disagreement. Mice, once amiable neighbors, turned upon each other with teeth and claws, their once harmonious existence shattered by the specter of overcrowding. Despite the abundance of resources, the overcrowded conditions led to a decline in reproduction rates. Female mice became less likely to conceive and nurture offspring, contributing to a stagnant or declining population growth rate. Eventually, the population of mice in Universe 25 experienced a dramatic collapse. Despite the availability of food and water, the social stresses caused by overcrowding led to a breakdown of normal behavior and reproduction, ultimately resulting in a sharp decline in population size. The experiment ended when the population of mice reached a critical point characterized by a high mortality rate, social disintegration, and a lack of viable reproduction. Calhoun described this phase as the "behavioral sink," where individuals withdrew from social interactions and exhibited dysfunctional behaviors.

And then, as if fate itself had decreed it, Universe 25 reached a precipice—a point of no return. The once bustling population dwindled, decimated by a cocktail of social decay and psychological malaise. In the unfortunate conclusion of Calhoun's experiment, a poignant truth echoed that transcended the boundaries of mere rodents. This truth spoke of the fragility of social bonds and the harrowing depths of the human condition.

"There have been approximately a hundred billion people who have ever lived on Earth. To understand how many potential human beings could have existed, we need to look at the number of possible combinations of genes that can create an authentic human, which is an incredibly large number. It is larger than 10 to the 30th power, which is a billion-trillion-trillion times larger than the 100 billion people who have ever lived.

Therefore, the fact that you are alive today is a gift of chance, as most people who could exist mathematically will never exist and will never experience the wonders of life, such as breath-

ing air, observing sunsets, and gazing into the night sky. As Richard Dawkins eloquently put it, 'We are going to die, and that makes us the lucky ones. Most people are never going to die because they are never going to be born. The potential people who could have been here in my place but who will, in fact, never see the light of day outnumber the sand grains of Arabia. Certainly, those unborn ghosts include greater poets than Keats and scientists greater than Newton. We know this because the set of possible people allowed by our DNA so massively exceeds the set of actual people. In the teeth of these stupefying odds, it is you and I, in our ordinariness, that are here. We privileged few, who won the lottery of birth against all odds, how dare we whine at our inevitable return to that prior state from which the vast majority have never stirred?'"
- Neil deGrasse Tyson.

We're instructed to pair up for procreation, but love itself seems inconsequential when viewed against the vastness of the galaxy. Without your parents meeting, you wouldn't exist; in fact, the same goes for any of your great-great-great-great-grandparents' ancestors back through generations. Each individual in the universe is the product of unique unions, yet ultimately insignificant. Our lifespan is fleeting, and the laws of physics confine us to this solar system. According to scientific predictions, roughly five billion years from now, the sun is expected to grow into a red giant, which will cause the complete annihilation of our planet and the extinction of all life forms inhabiting it. This cataclysmic event will likely occur eons after humans have vanished, joining dinosaurs and other extinct species. We're a minuscule blip in a universe oblivious to our existence. Some might label me a nihilist; our existence holds no inherent meaning and will fade into obscurity. Yet, despite this existential insignificance, we find meaning in each other, for the essence of life; which to me, lies in simply living a story that you can make sense of. By having no glorious purpose, you have the gift of finding purpose by loving and loving. This is existentialism.

Consider the following progression through History: From the emergence of Hunter-Gatherer societies to the advent of Agriculture, humanity advanced over a span of more than a hundred thousand years. Transitioning from the Agricultural Revolution to the Industrial Age took several millennia. Surprisingly, the leap from the Industrial Age to the Atomic Age occurred within a mere two hundred years. Subsequently, in just a few decades, humanity entered the Information Age, displaying an unprecedented ability to rapidly accelerate progress. Among the 2.13 million species that have inhabited Earth, none have demonstrated such remarkable developmental speed. It's conceivable that Homo sapiens, with their rapid advancement, may have hindered the development of other intelligent life forms. Our civilization's technological prowess is on track to far surpass the state-of-the-art advancements of the early 21st century, driven by the acceleration of advancements like Quantum Computing and Artificial Intelligence. These transformative changes are reshaping global dynamics, defying prediction.

Future generations may view our current concerns—political disputes, mortality, and diplomatic challenges—with the same indifference with which we regard our ancestors' struggles. In the grand reinterpretation of history, most individuals will fade into obscurity, their existence barely remembered after a few generations. As time marches on, memories diminish, and people move forward with their lives. So why do we pursue projects aimed at achieving immortality, seeking external validation, or striving for lofty reputations when, ultimately, our lives seem fleeting and unimportant?

Instead of pondering our existence's purpose when we seem inconsequential on a global or cosmic scale, akin to a rodent within its colony amidst countless rat colonies worldwide, the role of that and within the broader context of all 21.3 million species is negligible. Individual mice, or even mundane roles like a local gym's pool boy or a retired postman rendered obsolete by automation, contribute insignificantly to the world's grand scheme. Given this perspective, what rationale underlies our belief in our own significance or impact? What propels humans toward such a narcissistic sense of entitlement, leading us to genuinely believe we can alter humanity's trajectory within our mere 80-100 years on this planet? Is it the next step of Maslow's hierarchy of needs, transcending physiological necessities and pursuing self-esteem? Or are we simply cogs of the more elaborate system, working towards our impending collective demise? Are we oblivious to The Turnings and The Changing World Order? Are we mice in our own 'Experiment 25', destroying the Utopian planet we came to inherit?

Historically, we have developed an 'Us vs Them' mentality within our psyche, like the rodents mentioned above, creating a perception of any and all events as either an affirmation or a threat to one's own perspective of themselves. If something incredible happens to you, it is because of your own merits; however, if anything remotely unpleasant is experienced, it can be of no fault of your own but rather a societal or third-party coalition to torpedo your ascension, a victimhood chic of sorts. This entitlement to a false sense of glorious purpose, an existential burden of exceptionalism, is a mere replica of instant gratification. Proper measurement of self-worth comes not only from the acceptance of all the great things in your life as a result of your own actions but also from the realization that the bad is also a creation of your own doing.

At a young age, we tend to be influenced more by anger and resentment toward the big evil world for all the problems around us. The slightest inconvenience may resonate with a traumatic magnitude in children and adolescents who experience different levels of emotional affect. Like most youngsters, we tend to develop an uninformed assumption of an inability to resolve our own problems. The children that grow up facing losses and hardship - maybe not traumatic stress - but an appropriate level of misfortune, grow to realize that problems can be overcome as they experience a mixture of success and failure. The younglings that grow up shielded by their guardians or fail to experience any positive outcome to repeated harmful exposure will develop learned helplessness due to an underdeveloped locus of control, blaming others for their misfortune, the entitled victim.

To compensate for this severe lack of self-efficacy, we adopt one of two mentalities: that one is superior to others and deserves to be treated as special, or that one is unfairly disadvantaged by others and, therefore, requires special treatment. Opposite in perspective, but the same self-centered perception. This, by no means, is an attempt to remove the severity of specific problems one may have. At the same time, it is not to reinforce that some issues deserve more attention than others. It is the realization that no one is special and everyone has problems. Your ability to handle said problems and the consequence of your particular issues on the grand scale of the world should be the determining factor of self-esteem and your overall sense of purpose, i.e., self-actualization.

In this internal thought process, we must acknowledge the opportunity cost, the next best alternative forgone in our tyrannical pursuit of exceptionalism. To be incredible at one thing, you must forgo the next best alternative. In his mission to make humanity a multi-planetary species, Elon Musk has sacrificed material and familial pleasures such as super-yachts or mega-mansions, time with his children or spouses, and the time he could travel the world and live 'his best life.' To him, his perceived contribution to this world justifies the opportunity cost, sacrifice, and suffering. To a celibate religious monk, his devotion to god supersedes his desire to experience private ownership and a marital bond. Norio Suzuki, the Japanese explorer, forgave education in pursuit of exploratory experience. In the grand scheme of things, did the discovery of Hiroo Onoda, a soldier trapped in the jungles of Asia, affect the course of humanity? Probably not, but it did provide an awe-inspiring story in my book, and maybe it inspired a few people along the way, like the butterfly effect, encouraging prisoners of the Cave, as theorized by Plato, to escape and find enlightenment.

As comedian Jimmy Carr quite eloquently puts it, the modern world suffers from life dysmorphia. We've all heard of body dysmorphia, which is defined by a constant fixation on a perceived or minor flaw in one's appearance. There is also a condition called gender dysmorphia in which an individual experiences a notable dichotomy between their expressed or experienced gender and the sex they were assigned at birth. We, the global masses, all share a sense of life dysmorphia, assuming that our lives are somewhat terrible and sub-par to others. No matter how great your situation may be, you will always get used to it, and the grass may be greener elsewhere. Before the Industrial Revolution, no one ever experienced a hot show, television, or Wi-Fi/Bluetooth technology. Victorian-era children would go into shock if they were exposed to a football stadium, sororities, hot goat yoga, or an EDM concert. The next time we complain about the lukewarm water of our specifically designed shower head that emulates rainfall, remember that the simpler times of the past that we have come to idealize came with far fewer luxuries than those we take for granted in today's day and age. The more recent generations experience a standard of living in the top 0.01% of humans to have ever existed. Yet, we are the most miserable generation because we fail to acknowledge how incredibly great we have it in our abundance of caloric intake, diminishing mortality rates, and unprecedented levels of amusement we receive every second of every waking minute of our lives. Our existence has never been objectively better but is subjectively worse. The nature of humanity is memetic; how happy you are may be the result of your quality of life, tainted by the envy you feel from another's state of being.

We are all, or at least 99% of us, average joes that will be forgotten in the span of three to four turnings. The world is littered with extraordinary people who consistently achieve incredible feats. These achievements are broadcasted, studied, reiterated, and etched into our history. We will always try to mimic them, desire what others have, and crave for our stories to be told for generations to come. But like the quote from the inception of this chapter: "History isn't fact. It's a narrative, one carefully curated and shaped. Under the right scribe, a hero becomes a villain, a victory becomes a tragedy, and a lie becomes the truth. The storyteller controls the narrative. History is written by the victors, but it is rewritten by those who seek the truth."

Every person you pass by is living a life as complex and vivid as your own. They have their ambitions, friends, routines, worries, and quirks that may be radically divergent from your own. Their sonder lives are an epic story that continues invisibly around you, similar to an anthill sprawling underground, with intricate passageways leading to thousands of other imagined realities you may never know existed. You might appear in their lives once, like a background character sipping coffee, a blur of traffic on the highway, or a lighted window at dusk. We all play a small yet crucial role in the progress of humanity; although it may not be visible to you up close.

By taking a step back, you can see your role in your immediate community and how your community affects you. If you try to further your viewpoint, you can gain an understanding of the larger systems of social constructivism that make the world function. This understanding can reveal the truth about changing world orders and the cyclical nature of the four turnings. Like the rats of Universe 25, we are not in control. So what is the point? Do we just blindly accept the inevitable demise we know is coming? Yes! We are the apex predators of Earth because we tear ourselves down to rebuild a better version. We collectively, unintentionally, repeatedly do this. We can't stop it, and we shouldn't stop it. A species that fails to evolve goes extinct. The only thing you can do in this grand scheme of things is to simply exist, with a purpose that you have to assign for yourself, taking full accountability for your state of existence. This is existential theory.

Don't waste your life trying to live another individual's narrative. Your existence is unique to the billions of trillions of people who have or could have ever existed. Your purpose in life is to write your own history as a hero, the protagonist, romanticized, and not the villain; the victor and not the victim, the truth and not a lie you tell yourself to rest easy at night. Your glorious story may not be filled with exotic possessions, interplanetary journeys, relationships, fame, money, power, or immortal projects; you may not even have a tombstone to mark your presence on this planet. The one thing you have complete autonomy over is your narrative. Isn't that the whole point of our insignificant existence? To experience time to the best of your ability, with the things that matter most to you, for no one else but yourself.

Individuals come into existence first and then define themselves through actions and choices. There is no predetermined essence or purpose to human life. Instead, we create our own essence through the choices made at every crossroad. Every person has the freedom to choose their path in life. However, with this freedom comes the responsibility to take ownership of one's choices and actions as they shape one's reality. Existential dread stems from realizing our ultimate isolation and the lack of inherent meaning in life. Living authentically means being true to oneself and one's values rather than conforming to societal norms or expectations. Authentic living involves embracing freedom, making meaningful choices, and taking responsibility for your existence.

"The proper function of man is to live,
not to exist. I shall not waste my days
in trying to prolong them.
I shall use my time."
- Jack London.

–The End–

ABOUT THE AUTHOR

Vipulesh Thiyagarajah is a Sri Lankan business leader based in Colombo. 'Sonder' is his debut novel.

"The idea of people reading my writing is quite terrifying! It's pretty vulnerable to put your thoughts out there for everyone to judge. But in "Sonder: An Existential Manifesto," I do my best to share the nuances of a full-blown existential crisis in my twenties. It wasn't always pretty, but it introduced me to a whole new perspective on life.This book isn't just me rambling about the meaning of life (though, okay, maybe a little); It's about digging into the big questions I wrestled with, both scientifically and philosophically, rediscovering that childlike sense of wonder in a world that can sometimes feel a bit overwhelming."

Connect with the Author by scanning the QR Code below:

ACKNOWLEDGEMENTS

This book wouldn't exist without the unwavering support of an extraordinary group of people who helped turn the cluster of words on my laptop into the manuscript it is today. First and foremost, my deepest gratitude goes to my parents. Their encouragement, patience, and support through the publishing process got me through the moments of doubt.

Thanks to Elizabeth Long for her invaluable feedback. Miss Kamini Perera and Paul Byatt, I have appreciated their unyielding advice, teachings, and guidance since I was an annoying little kid. Your contributions have not only shaped this book but also my personal growth and learning as a writer.

I am deeply grateful to Nishara Fernando and Rishard Rassool for their valuable edits and commitment to shaping this manuscript. Their contributions have significantly enhanced the quality of the book, making it a more polished and refined piece of work. A heartfelt thank you to Jasmine Markandu, whose relentless help has been a game-changer, going above and beyond what I could have ever hoped for.

Finally, to all the people who contributed to this book in any way, shape, or form, whether it was by providing moral support, helping with research, or simply being a sounding board for my ideas, you all kept me sane and made my life easier in trying to get this book out. Thank you.

BIBLIOGRAPHY

Chapter 1

Maddocks, J. (2020). *Future colors*. Retrieved June 23, 2024, from https://core.ac.uk/download/326604498.pdf

Singh, H. (2022, March 24). It is the task of the enlightened. Retrieved June 23, 2024, from https://iamhimanshusingh2022.wordpress.com/2022/03/24/it-is-the-task-of-the-enlightened/

Spellbound. (2020, November). Is your threat brain always. *Psychology Today*. Retrieved June 23, 2024, from https://www.psychologytoday.com/intl/blog/spellbound/202011/is-your-threat-brain-always

Spellbound. (2021, March). The curse of consciousness. *Psychology Today*. Retrieved June 23, 2024, from https://www.psychologytoday.com/intl/blog/spellbound/202103/the-curse-consciousness

The blessing of being and the curse of consciousness. (n.d.). *Thrive Global*. Retrieved June 23, 2024, from https://community.thriveglobal.com/the-blessing-of-being-and-the-curse-of-consciousness/#:~:text=The%20unbounded%20balance%20

between%20the%20blessing%20and%20the%20curse.&-
text=Our%20own%20minds%20can%20create,being%20
cursed%20all%20the%20time.

Chapter 2

Aphantasia Network. (n.d.). Vividness of Visual Imagery Questionnaire. Retrieved June 23, 2024, from https://aphantasia.com/vviq/

Brooks, A. C. (n.d.). PANAS lesson plan. Retrieved June 23, 2024, from https://arthurbrooks.com/hubfs/PANAS%20Lesson%20Plan-1.pdf

Brooks, A. C. (2023, September). Harvard's Arthur C. Brooks on the secrets to happiness at work. Harvard Business Review. https://hbr.org/2023/09/harvards-arthur-c-brooks-on-the-secrets-to-happiness-at-work

Diener, E., Lucas, R. E., & Scollon, C. N. (2006). Beyond the hedonic treadmill: Revising the adaptation theory of well-being. American Psychologist. Retrieved June 23, 2024, from http://labs.psychology.illinois.edu/~ediener/Documents/Diener-Lucas-Scollon_2006.pdf

McMahon, D. M. (n.d.). Happiness: A history. Retrieved June 23, 2024, from https://qz.com/958677/happiness-a-history-author-darrin-m-mcmahon-explains-when-the-idea-of-happiness-was-invented

Verywell Mind. (n.d.). Wants vs. needs. Retrieved June 23, 2024, from https://www.verywellmind.com/what-is-happiness-4869755#:~:text=Joy%3A%20A%20often%20relatively%20brief,in%20something%20that%20you%20have

Chapter 3

Modern Husbands. (n.d.). 6 tips to find happiness and avoid a mid-life crisis. Retrieved June 23, 2024, from https://www.modernhusbands.com/post/how-to-be-happier

BMJ. (2008, December 9). Juliet Walker: What's new on bmj.com. The BMJ. Retrieved June 23, 2024, from https://blogs.bmj.com/bmj/2008/12/09/juliet-walker-on-whats-new-this-week-on-bmjcom/

Business Insider. (2012, July). Jim Rohn: You're the average of the five people you spend the most time with. Retrieved June 23, 2024, from https://www.businessinsider.com/jim-rohn-youre-the-average-of-the-five-people-you-spend-the-most-time-with-2012-7

CNBC. (2023, February 10). 85-year Harvard study found the secret to a long, happy, and successful life. Retrieved June 23, 2024, from https://www.cnbc.com/2023/02/10/85-year-harvard-study-found-the-secret-to-a-long-happy-and-successful-life.html#:~:text=The%20No.%201%20key%20to,happy%20life%3A%20%27Social%20fitness%27&text=To%20

make%20sure%20your%20relationships,will%20take%20 care%20of%20themselves.

Harvard T.H. Chan School of Public Health. (2023, February 27). The good life: A discussion with Dr. Robert Waldinger. Retrieved June 23, 2024, from https:// www.hsph.harvard.edu/health-happiness/2023/02/27/ the-good-life-a-discussion-with-dr-robert-waldinger/

Internet and Psychiatry. (n.d.). Science declares happiness is con- tagious. Retrieved June 23, 2024, from https://www.intern- etandpsychiatry.com/wp/topics/other-psychiatric-disorders/ science-declares-happiness-is-contagious/

Law of Averages | The Heretic. (2016). Retrieved June 23, 2024, from https://theheretic.org/2016/law-of-averages/

Morsodifame. (n.d.). Traduzione everyone you meet is fighting a hard battle be kind always. Retrieved June 23, 2024, from https://morsodifame.com/traduzione-everyone-you-meet-is- fighting-a-hard-battle-be-kind-always.html

Modern Husbands. (n.d.). 6 tips to find happiness and avoid a mid-life crisis. Retrieved June 23, 2024, from https://www. modernhusbands.com/post/how-to-be-happier

Thinking Big Coaching. (n.d.). The secret behind why "We are the average of the five people ...". Retrieved June 23, 2024, from https://www.thinkingbigcoaching.com/blog/mirrorneurons

The Heretic. (2016). Law of averages. Retrieved June 23, 2024, from https://theheretic.org/2016/law-of-averages/

Chapter 4

Anastasia, N., & Malelak, M. I. (2019). Effects of personality trait in financial risk tolerance investor in Surabaya. Retrieved June 23, 2024, from https://core.ac.uk/download/225544409.pdf

Christianity in the Renaissance | Faith in Action AZ. (n.d.). Humanism. Retrieved June 23, 2024, from https://faithinactionaz.org/christian-history/christianity-in-the-renaissance/

Clear, James. (2018). *Atomic Habits: an easy & proven way to build good habits & break bad ones* (PDF ed.). New York: Avery.

Dexus. (n.d.). Maintaining your sanity in isolation. Retrieved June 23, 2024, from https://www.dexus.com/dexus-insights/the-loneliness-pandemic

EduTinker. (n.d.). Discipline and its importance in life. Retrieved June 23, 2024, from https://edutinker.com/glossary/discipline-and-its-importance-in-life/

Eastside Alumni. (n.d.). Imposter Syndrome: Alumni reflections with Ashley Vega, '15. Retrieved June 23, 2024, from https://www.alumni.eastside.org/post/imposter-syndrome-alumni-reflections-with-ashely-vega-15

Escola de Inglês. (n.d.). Self Actualization: Total commitment. Retrieved June 23, 2024, from https://www.escoladeingles.net/post/total-commitment

Ince, M. (2023). Examining the role of motivation, attitude, and self-efficacy beliefs in shaping secondary school students' academic achievement in science course. Sustainability, 15(15), 11612.

Maslow, A. (n.d.). Hierarchy of needs. Verywell Mind. Retrieved June 23, 2024, from https://www.verywellmind.com/what-is-maslows-hierarchy-of-needs-4136760

Max Zsol. (n.d.). Illusionary effect: Repetition Bias. Retrieved June 23, 2024, from https://maxzsol.com/repetition-bias

Takimoto, T. (n.d.). 9+ Tatsuhiko Takimoto quotes and sayings. QUOTLR. Retrieved June 23, 2024, from https://quotlr.com/author/tatsuhiko-takimoto

The Behavioral Scientist. (n.d.). Illusory Truth Effect. Retrieved June 23, 2024, from https://www.thebehavioralscientist.com/glossary/illusory-truth-effect

Larry Summers, former President of Harvard University. (n.d.). A monologue by Larry Summers, former President of Harvard University, stated on a panel at the All-In Summit.

Maslow's hierarchy of needs. (n.d.). *Verywell Mind.* https://www.verywellmind.com/what-is-maslows-hierarchy-of-needs-4136760

Christianity in the Renaissance. (n.d.). *Faith in Action AZ*. https://faithinactionaz.org/christian-history/christianity-in-the-renaissance/

Total commitment. (n.d.). *Escola de Ingles*. https://www.escolade-ingles.net/post/total-commitment

Maintaining your sanity in isolation. (n.d.). *Dexus*. https://www.dexus.com/dexus-insights/the-loneliness-pandemic

Imposter Syndrome: Alumni reflections with Ashely Vega, '15. (n.d.). *Eastside Alumni*. https://www.alumni.eastside.org/post/imposter-syndrome-alumni-reflections-with-ashely-vega-15

Discipline and its importance in life. (n.d.). *eduTinker*. https://edutinker.com/glossary/discipline-and-its-importance-in-life/

Zsol, M. (n.d.). *Repetition bias*. https://maxzsol.com/repetition-bias

Illusory truth effect. (n.d.). *The Behavioral Scientist*. https://www.thebehavioralscientist.com/glossary/illusory-truth-effect

Clear, J. *Atomic Habits*.

Tatsuhiko Takimoto quotes and sayings. (n.d.). *Quotlr*. https://quotlr.com/author/tatsuhiko-takimoto

Seligman, M. *Learned helplessness*.

Anastasia, N., & Malelak, M. I. (2019). Effects of personality trait in financial risk tolerance investor in Surabaya. https://core.ac.uk/download/225544409.pdf

İnce, M. (2023). Examining the role of motivation, attitude, and self-efficacy beliefs in shaping secondary school students' academic achievement in science course. *Sustainability, 15*(15), 11612.

Chapter 5

National Center for Biotechnology Information. (n.d.). PMC Article. Retrieved June 23, 2024, from https://www.ncbi.nlm.nih.gov/pmc/articles/PMC2568977/

The Knowledge. (n.d.). The backwards law. Retrieved June 23, 2024, from https://theknowledge.io/the-backwards-law/

Einzelganger. (n.d.). The backwards law. Retrieved June 23, 2024, from https://einzelganger.co/the-backwards-law/

Travers, M. (2024, March 3). A psychologist explains misalignment burnout: When your job isn't your purpose. Forbes. Retrieved June 23, 2024, from https://www.forbes.com/sites/traversmark/2024/03/03/a-psychologist-explains-misalignment-burnout-when-your-job-isnt-your-purpose/#:~:text=Misalignment%20burnout%20decreases%20organizational%20performance,affecting%20team%20dynamics%20and%20collaboration.

Williamson, C. (n.d.). 3 Minute Monday - Sacrifice, Smart Virgins and Socrates | Chris Williamson. Retrieved June 23, 2024, from https://chriswillx.com/3-minute-monday-sacrifice-smart-virgins-and-socrates/?utm_source=rss&utm_

medium=rss&utm_campaign=3-minute-monday-sacri-fice-smart-virgins-and-socrates

Necrolog. (2014). Fortean Times, (312), 22-23.

Luxury Daily. (n.d.). Audi highlights passion, progress in new film series. Retrieved June 23, 2024, from https://www.luxurydaily.com/audi-highlights-passion-progress-in-new-film-series/

The Chronicle. (2013, June 24). Retrieved June 23, 2024, from https://core.ac.uk/download/519838997.pdf

Dostoevsky, F. (n.d.). A man who lies to himself, and believes his own.... Retrieved June 23, 2024, from https://www.azquotes.com/quote/588022

Verywell Mind. (n.d.). Will Reaching a Goal Make You Happy? Arrival Fallacy. Retrieved June 23, 2024, from https://www.verywellmind.com/what-is-arrival-fallacy-6561079

Playful Humans. (n.d.). Backward Law: Learning to Play for a Living. Retrieved June 23, 2024, from https://playfulhumans.com/play-for-a-living/

Stokes, S., Kanwar, R., Jain, S., Adapa, K., Meltzer-Brody, S., & Mazur, L. (2021). Hospitalist burnout and sociotechnical factors contributing to workplace stress. ISE; Industrial and Systems Engineering at Work, 53(2), 28-33.

SEOmator. (2023). Blogging Statistics in 2023: Revealing Critical Stats Behind the Power of Digital Storytelling. Retrieved June 23, 2024, from https://seomator.com/blog/blogging-statistics

School of Theatre and Dance, Illinois State University. (1988). 1988 Illinois Shakespeare Festival Program. Retrieved June 23, 2024, from https://core.ac.uk/download/516413362.pdf

Ballinger, A. J. (1995). Religious Dissidents of the Soviet Union from 1962 to 1985: Baptists and Catholics. Retrieved June 23, 2024, from https://oatd.org/oatd/record?record=oai:content.library.ccsu.edu:ccsutheses%2F2689

National Center for Biotechnology Information. (n.d.). PMC Article. National Center for Biotechnology Information. Retrieved June 23, 2024, from https://www.ncbi.nlm.nih.gov/pmc/articles/PMC2568977/

The Knowledge. (n.d.). The backwards law. Retrieved June 23, 2024, from https://theknowledge.io/the-backwards-law/

Einzelganger. (n.d.). The backwards law. Retrieved June 23, 2024, from https://einzelganger.co/the-backwards-law/

Travers, M. (2024, March 3). A psychologist explains misalignment burnout: When your job isn't your purpose. Forbes. Retrieved June 23, 2024, from https://www.forbes.com/sites/traversmark/2024/03/03/a-psychologist-explains-misalignment-burnout-when-your-job-isnt-your-purpose/

Williamson, C. (n.d.). 3 Minute Monday - Sacrifice, smart virgins, and Socrates. Chris Williamson. Retrieved June 23, 2024, from https://chriswillx.com/3-minute-monday-sacrifice-smart-virgins-and-socrates/?utm_source=rss&utm_

medium=rss&utm_campaign=3-minute-monday-sacri-fice-smart-virgins-and-socrates

Necrolog. (2014). Fortean Times, (312), 22-23.

Luxury Daily. (n.d.). Audi highlights passion, progress in new film series. Retrieved June 23, 2024, from https://www.luxurydai-ly.com/audi-highlights-passion-progress-in-new-film-series/

The Chronicle. (2013, June 24). Retrieved June 23, 2024, from https://core.ac.uk/download/519838997.pdf

Dostoevsky, F. (n.d.). A man who lies to himself, and believes his own. AZ Quotes. Retrieved June 23, 2024, from https://www.azquotes.com/quote/588022

Verywell Mind. (n.d.). Will reaching a goal make you happy? Arrival fallacy. Retrieved June 23, 2024, from https://www.verywellmind.com/what-is-arrival-fallacy-6561079

Playful Humans. (n.d.). Backward law: Learning to play for a living. Retrieved June 23, 2024, from https://playfulhumans.com/play-for-a-living/

Stokes, S., Kanwar, R., Jain, S., Adapa, K., Meltzer-Brody, S., & Mazur, L. (2021). Hospitalist burnout and sociotechnical factors contributing to workplace stress. ISE; Industrial and Systems Engineering at Work, 53(2), 28-33.

SEOmator. (2023). Blogging statistics in 2023: Revealing critical stats behind the power of digital storytelling. Retrieved June 23, 2024, from https://seomator.com/blog/blogging-statistics

School of Theatre and Dance, Illinois State University. (1988). 1988 Illinois Shakespeare Festival Program. Retrieved June 23, 2024, from https://core.ac.uk/download/516413362.pdf

Ballinger, A. J. (1995). Religious dissidents of the Soviet Union from 1962 to 1985: Baptists and Catholics. Retrieved June 23, 2024, from https://oatd.org/oatd/record?record=oai:content.library.ccsu.edu:ccsutheses%2F2689

Chapter 6

Fortune Unmasked Worldwide. (n.d.). Mimetics. Retrieved June 23, 2024, from https://www.fortuneunmasked.com/category/mimetics/

Harari, Y. N. (2014). Sapiens: A brief history of humankind. Retrieved from [insert full URL]

Drapal, A. (2021, July 29). Invisible hand. Retrieved June 23, 2024, from https://andrejdrapal.com/2021/07/29/invisible-hand/

Fortune Unmasked Worldwide. (n.d.). Mimetics. Retrieved June 23, 2024, from https://www.fortuneunmasked.com/category/mimetics/

Drapal, A. (2021, July 29). Invisible hand. Retrieved June 23, 2024, from https://andrejdrapal.com/2021/07/29/invisible-hand/

Mimetic Theory. (n.d.). What it is. Retrieved June 23, 2024, from https://mimetictheory.com/what-it-is-2/

Violence and Religion. (n.d.). Mimetic theory. Retrieved June 23, 2024, from https://violenceandreligion.com/mimetic-theory/

Zhang, Z., Zhou, F., & Ning, H. (n.d.). When six degrees of separation meets online social networks: How low can the degree be? Asymmetric Wisdom. Retrieved June 23, 2024, from https://asymmetricwisdom.medium.com/what-the-werewolf-game-teaches-us-about-us-09ffe0d812b6

Oxford Reference. (n.d.). Information asymmetry. Retrieved June 23, 2024, from https://www.oxfordreference.com/display/10.1093/oi/authority.20110803095637587

Chapter 7

Diener, E., Lucas, R. E., & Scollon, C. N. (2006). Beyond the hedonic treadmill: Revising the adaptation theory of well-being. http://labs.psychology.illinois.edu/~ediener/Documents/Diener-Lucas-Scollon_2006.pdf

Harari, Y. N. (2015). Sapiens: A brief history of humankind. Harper.

Investopedia. (n.d.). Veblen good. https://www.investopedia.com/terms/v/veblen-good.asp

Yeo, A. (n.d.). Perception is projection. https://www.ariesyeo.com/perception-is-projection

Chapter 8

Calhoun, J. B. (1962). Universe 25 Experiment. Journal of Experimental Psychology, 63(3), 1-10. doi: 10.1037/h0044446

Howe, N., & Strauss, W. (2023). *The fourth turning is here: what the seasons of history tell us about how and when this crisis will end* (First Simon & Schuster hardcover edition.). Simon & Schuster.

Dalio, R. (2021). *Principles for dealing with the changing world order.* Avid Reader Press.

Guastello, S. J., Dooley, K. J., & Goldstein, J. A. (1995). *Chaos, organizational theory, and organizational development.* In F. D. Abraham & A. R. Gilgen (Eds.), Chaos theory in psychology (pp. 267–278). Praeger Publishers/Greenwood Publishing Group.